The BEAUTY of SOULS

Praise for *The Beauty of Souls*

Mark Scott's careful, ruminative readings of Marilynne Robinson's celebrated novels offer much more than literary or theological analysis: they recover a nascent spirituality. A Robinsonian spirituality, he argues, follows no singular path, since it must accommodate our unique pasts, personal pains, and yearning for authenticity. Yet, her overarching theme, what Scott calls "the beauty of souls," connects us through a brokenness overcome by our shared participation in the boundless beauty of the Eternal. By the time readers have finished Scott's peerless study, not only will they understand Robinson's characters much better: they will be better equipped to carry on the work of soul craft in their own lives.

—Brett Malcolm Grainger, associate professor of theology and religious studies, Villanova University

In the nineteenth century, Americans looked to figures such as Emerson, Thoreau, and Whitman to help them see beauty and discover the human soul, but in our own times one greater than any of them has arisen. Marilynne Robinson is the voice we need to truly see ourselves, our neighbors, and our world. Mark S. M. Scott is himself a wise, old soul, and this book is nothing less than an invitation to celebrate humanity in its fullness.

—Timothy Larsen, Carolyn and Fred McManis Professor of Christian Thought, Wheaton College, and editor of *Balm in Gilead: A Theological Dialogue with Marilynne Robinson*

Scott's *The Beauty of Souls* presents a carefully insightful and intricately comprehensive close reading of all Marilynne Robinson's novels. For this alone it deserves praise. But *The Beauty of Souls* is more than just a literary analysis: it is also a spiritually attentive and deeply compassionate theology of human personhood and divine beauty.

—Matthew Ichihashi Potts, Plummer Professor of Christian Morals and Pusey Minister in the Memorial Church, Harvard University

The Beauty of Souls provides an interpretive map for curious readers, those wanting to explore some of the most enduring topics in Marilynne Robinson's writing: namely, the integrative relationship between human souls, beauty, and lived experience. After giving us robust insight into these matters through Robinson's essays, Mark S. M. Scott guides us through the theological and aesthetic nuances of her fictional worlds—places where wandering souls are beautiful, wounded, and embattled—but this book does even more. In our own noisy world, Scott's gentle voice helps us begin to recognize and reclaim the interior landscape of our lives. By the end of this journey, readers will see that each soul—whether encountered in the self, in others, or in representations of art—is a created gift, something as tangible and irreducible as a resonating symphony or a luminous painting.

—Chad Wriglesworth, associate professor of English, St. Jerome's University

The BEAUTY of SOULS

Aesthetic Encounters with MARILYNNE ROBINSON

MARK S. M. SCOTT

Fortress Press
Minneapolis

THE BEAUTY OF SOULS
Aesthetic Encounters with Marilynne Robinson

30 29 28 27 26 25 24 1 2 3 4 5 6 7 8 9

Library of Congress Cataloging-in-Publication Data

Names: Scott, Mark S. M., author.
Title: The beauty of souls : aesthetic encounters with Marilynne Robinson / Mark S. M. Scott.
Description: Minneapolis : Fortress Press, [2025] | Includes bibliographical references and index.
Identifiers: LCCN 2024032756 (print) | LCCN 2024032757 (ebook) | ISBN 9781506495644 (print) | ISBN 9781506495651 (ebook)
Subjects: LCSH: Philosophical theology. | Christian philosophy. | Spirituality.
Classification: LCC BT40 .S368 2025 (print) | LCC BT40 (ebook) | DDC 230.01--dc23/eng/20240917
LC record available at https://lccn.loc.gov/2024032756
LC ebook record available at https://lccn.loc.gov/2024032757

Cover image: Sunrise on Landscape, stock illustration by CSA Images/Getty Images
Cover design: Kristin Miller

Print ISBN: 978-1-5064-9564-4
eBook ISBN: 978-1-5064-9565-1

To the Rev. Dr. John Nixon McMillan
(July 17, 1948–August 26, 2024).
A sterling soul.

We thank You for his beautiful mind,
his beautiful life, and the music
that flowed through him.

Contents

Acknowledgments

I wish to thank my colleagues at the Centre for Studies in Religion and Society at the University of Victoria (British Columbia, Canada) where I undertook research for this study as a visiting research fellow from January 1 to August 31, 2022. It was virtual, yet vital. Thanks also to my undergraduate and graduate students who read Robinson's writings with me in various settings.

Preface

Pulitzer Prize–winning author Marilynne Robinson compares literature to music. Her fictional characters have distinctive melodies that repeat with slight variations as their stories unfold. If we listen closely, an ethereal, eccentric, euphonious score emerges. It is a literary opera with deep spiritual overtones. Like operas, her fiction exhibits a wide spectrum of human emotion: love, joy, anger, sadness, regret, despair, and hope. In my study, I try to "listen" to the music of her novels through the theoretical lens of the beauty of souls, and then "sing" the music it elicits. In that sense, *The Beauty of Souls* is a spiritual duet between Robinson's literary opera and the music of my own soul where I harmonize with the main melodies of her novels. My study surfaces the latent spirituality of her novels and explores their implications and applications for the life of the soul. If it succeeds, it will stir the reader to celebrate the bounties of beauty in the world and stimulate further spiritual reflections.

The spiritual encounters from her fiction organically arise from her key characters, who share salient features. Most feel outside of the conventional rhythms of society. In *Housekeeping*, Sylvie eschews the societal expectations of a caregiver, while Ruth slowly drifts away from her school and her town to share in Sylvie's itinerant existence. In *Gilead*, Ames wanders in the evening, catching the scent of the night-cloaked trees, wondering about the lives of others, and returning home to listen to baseball on the radio until late into the night. In *Home*, Jack and Glory establish their own daily routines around the family home while viewing the outside world with apprehension and trepidation. In *Lila* and *Jack*, the title characters live outside of the standard economic and social structures. In various ways, they are all outsiders, operating on the edges or entirely outside of conventionality. That sense of marginalization inflects the spirituality that arises. They are all searching for a sense of home.

Moreover, all the major characters in her fiction are in a state of crisis physically, emotionally, or spiritually, or sometimes all three. Ruth and Lucille find themselves orphaned in a strange town when their mother Helen commits suicide. Ames faces declining health and his impending death while worrying about the new family he will leave behind. Lila begins her life abandoned, then abducted, then exploited, and finally ends up in Gilead where she cares for her dying husband and their young boy. Jack returns to Gilead in a last-ditch effort to make a life for his wife Della and their boy Robert. Glory returns home after a romantic misadventure, only to assume responsibility for her ailing father and wayward brother. They are all in crisis. Their fraught experiential contexts raise profound questions about suffering and meaning, about navigating existence, and about spiritual self-actualization.

As marginalized souls in various states of crisis, Robinson's characters tend to turn inward for solace, protection, and orientation. That inwardness naturally issues in an interior spirituality, a focus on the individual soul's personal road to floundering or flourishing. Inwardness does not, however, negate their engagement with the world. Her characters explore nature, reflect on relationships, live in society, and ponder the profound mysteries of existence. A Robinsonian spirituality, then, begins with the inward solitary soul and then expands outward. Unsurprisingly, then, her fiction awakens the soul to the wonder and beauty of the world; it does not, however, establish a community rule. Nevertheless, souls deeply attuned to beauty and enraptured by wonder will typically warm to other souls and enrich them through the activation of their spiritual capacities. Spiritual rejuvenation enhances community revitalization. Souls on fire light other souls. Souls ablaze change the world.

As we will see, Robinson's corpus underscores the need to take ownership of our souls, to claim them, to retrieve them from depersonalizing forces, and to express them authentically. We cannot outsource our soul-formation and soul-manifestation. God has given us unique souls that we must discover on our own and share with others. We cannot abdicate that responsibility to others, including clergy, family, and friends. They cannot tell us who we are spiritually because they cannot access the mysterious depths of our souls. Many of them can guide us on our spiritual journey, but the journey is ultimately ours. Spiritual self-discovery involves coming to terms with our past, confronting our pain, taking responsibility for our mistakes, knowing ourselves more deeply, and embracing our unique gifts. It is not an easy process, hence the desire to offload it to someone else or to evade it altogether. Robinson's writings, particularly her fiction, invite us to spiritual self-discovery.

Finally, the memorable souls we encounter in Robinson's fiction are multifaceted. The chapter titles for *Housekeeping*, *Gilead*, *Home*, *Lila*, and *Jack* foreground an essential aspect of their souls: wandering, beautiful, wounded, and embattled. These modifiers signal the spiritual focal points for our analysis but mislead if they are read as mutually exclusive. In fact, her characters share all these elements and many others to different degrees. They resist simple classification because the palette of Robinson's imagination utilizes many subtle shades beyond the primary colors. Likewise, our souls do not admit of simple, singular designations, which would flatten our histories, experiences, and potentialities.

Souls are kaleidoscopic, and their discovery depends on our ability to perceive and appreciate their complexity and to respect the mystery that lies beyond the visible, the impenetrable mystery of the hidden spaces of the soul. Robinson's fiction teaches us that there are no one-dimensional souls or simple spiritual storylines, only multifaceted souls in complex relations. That makes life with the self and others a wonderful adventure of spiritual discovery.

Introduction

> I can find nothing with which to compare the great beauty of a soul and its great capacity.
>
> —Teresa of Ávila, *Interior Castle*

Marilynne Robinson's fiction strikes deep spiritual chords. It awakens us to the beauty of the world through its delicate description of landscapes: from the depths of Fingerbone lake to the rising of the moon and setting of the sun over the prairies. More fundamentally, however, it spiritually sensitizes us to the beauty of souls through its intense concentration on the inner life of its characters. Whether in Ruth's ruminations about solitude or Reverend John Ames's celebration of life, Robinson's characters, with their emotional coherence, complexity, and contradictions, alert us to the reality of souls. As we encounter their carefully scribed souls, we have a heightened sense of *ourselves* as souls. Slowly, almost imperceptibly, her novels spiritually prepare us to recognize our own inwardness, to reclaim our beauty and the beauty of the world, and to reenter our own life stories with a renewed and expanded sense of self.

In this study, I argue that the beauty of souls constitutes the spiritual throughline of Robinson's writings. In different contexts and registers, her work affirms the dignity and value of souls as irreducibly unique and unconditionally loved, irrespective of their faults and failures. The beauty of souls, for Robinson, rests not on any false perfectionism, which always masks hidden imperfections, injuries, and insecurities, but rather on divine beauty. God, the source of all beauty, as Eternal Beauty, ceaselessly emanates beauty into creation, suffusing it throughout, shining most resplendently in the human soul, the pinnacle of creation. In its apprehensions, relationships, capacities, choices, and creations, the soul refracts the divine beauty, albeit imperfectly. For Robinson, the beauty of the soul sometimes lies deeply buried beneath compact layers of brokenness, bondage, and misfortune. Even there, damaged and defaced, it still shines.

From a literary standpoint, my study proposes a hermeneutical key to unlock the widespread appeal of her fiction. On the surface, her fiction seems unstructured, uneventful, and unconventional. Some find the lack of "action"—few car chases—and plot off-putting. On a narrative level, nothing really riveting happens. Yes, characters recall past excitements—train derailments, gun battles, and even a car chase—but nothing that serves as the kinetic fulcrum of the stories. No bombs are diffused, no lost relics found, no international plots exposed. In this sense, the stories often "don't go anywhere." Spiritually, however, the action is unrelenting, and the plot purposeful. Once readers realize the interior orientation of the novels, they find themselves pulled along by the undercurrent of beauty that lies beneath the placid surface. From a purely literary perspective, then, my study advances the thesis that the beauty of souls underlies her writings as its guiding spiritual motif.

But I want to go further with the deep-souled Robinson reader. I want to argue, in conjunction with my literary analysis, that her novels open spiritual vistas precisely because they are animated by the affirmation and actualization of the beauty of souls and the celebration of the "engrossing beauty of the vanishing present."[1] As we internalize her stories, we become more attentive to the beauty in ourselves and others. Robinson's fiction, then, inspires through its latent spirituality, which invites us to see her not just as a literary landmark, but also as a type of spiritual guide. Robinson serves as a guide to soul-discovery, soul-recovery, and soul-formation, and the secret to her popularity inside and outside of academic circles lies in her intellectual and imaginative surfacing of the spiritual questions around the soul's pivotal place in the cosmos. In a world increasingly graceless, hopeless, and soulless, her work refreshes and revitalizes like a gentle breeze in the stifling heat.

It is always timely to reclaim the soul. There is nothing new under the sun, even in a world with AI, social media, escalating geopolitical turmoil, and ever-evolving technological and medical advances. Systems have always pressed against souls, sometimes crushing them under their unrelenting weight. It was ever thus. Souls navigate the space between the self and the systems that ask—or demand—them to operate within their grand designs, always framed as benevolent and necessary. To insist on the singularity and preciousness of the soul subverts the systems that seek to coerce, control, and, ultimately, consume it. Systems depersonalize the self, and yet the self always exists within systems: national, political, legal, moral, educational, economic, familial, religious, and so on. They all exert themselves and pressure the soul to adhere to them with varying degrees of loyalty. "You're really just a number," spoken by so many current and former employees, expresses the dilemma well.

In Robinson's fiction, characters constantly collide with the systems that seek to absorb them into their structures, thereby engulfing their irreducibility through institutional conformity. Sylvie eschews traditional family roles and responsibilities. Ruth rejects school life. Ames feels outside of the conventional family life of his best friend and his own congregation, outside of its expectations when he marries Lila. Lila works on the outskirts of society. Jack and Della contravene its laws against interracial marriage.

Art mirrors life. We too find ourselves in constant tension with systems that erode our sense of self, sometimes to the point of erasure. Robinson's nonfiction and fiction enjoin us to reaffirm our souls, to know that we are not merely products of systems, not reducible to social or biological forces, and to cultivate beauty over a lifetime. It will force difficult decisions. She exhorts an unyielding and joyful affirmation of the self.

Souls also find and lose themselves in relationships with other souls in her fiction. Interpersonal relationships take center stage as the site of soul-formation. Families form souls in decisive ways, both through their faith and values as well as through their internal dynamics and dysfunctions. Those who do not align with the family ethos, or who feel outside of the circle, often wrestle with their sense of alienation or dislocation. Friendships also ground the characters in her novels, providing a sense of home for those who are emotionally, physically, or spiritually homeless. Finally, romantic relationships take the souls in her novels into exciting, dangerous, and often uncharted territory. The complexity of human relationships derives from the daily collision of souls, whose disparate histories, commitments, and sensibilities create conflict, confusion, and consternation. When hurt inevitably results from the friction, grace emerges as the only salve for wounded souls.

My study begins by establishing the thesis that the beauty of souls underwrites and animates her work. Chapters 1 and 2 detail the core concepts—soul and beauty—in Robinson's nonfiction, particularly her essays, mostly drawn from talks given all around the world. They delineate her preoccupation with the beauty of souls and identify promising heuristic sites, that is, focal points for reflection on the spiritual life. Chapters 3–6 explore the spiritual dimensions of each novel in order of publication, gleaning their rich insights into the beauty of souls and elucidating their spiritual implications. Each of these chapters begins with a brief synopsis before turning to the spiritual questions it surfaces and the insights it offers. These chapters create a dialogue between Robinson's fictional worlds and the real world, bridging them for the purpose of spiritual illumination and edification. The conclusion draws the threads together into a tapestry that integrates the major spiritual themes from the study.

It would be mistaken, however, to pitch Marilynne Robinson as a spiritual guru, someone around whom a school of religious instruction forms. Spiritual gurus teach systems of instruction and transformation through various practices, often from within religious organizations. Their systems frequently involve meditation and prayer, extensive study of religious texts, and living in communities of faith. Robinson, conversely, does not espouse any spiritual systems, offer any technical advice, or found any communities of faith. She does, however, open, soften, and enrich readers spiritually through the finely tuned characters of her fiction, and in that sense she functions—unwittingly—as a spiritual guide. A "Robinsonian spirituality," then, refers to the spiritual instincts, attitudes, and sensibilities that arise from her fiction, particularly attentiveness to the beauty of the mundane, the sacredness of the ordinary, and the mystery of existence.

The beauty of souls, then, will be the central motif of the study, its guiding refrain. It will move from argumentation to illustration to application. In the first two chapters, I analyze Robinson's arguments for the beauty of soul vis-à-vis its cultured dissenters, thereby establishing my theoretical orientation for reading her fiction, which I will argue illustrates her fundamental commitment to the beauty of souls. Then, as we delve into her fiction, we will discover her illustration of the beauty of souls in her characters and parse out the deep spiritual implications and applications. As a work of literary criticism, *The Beauty of Souls* offers a theoretical lens to interpret Robinson's writings, especially her fiction. As a work of spiritual lyricism, it explores her fiction not simply as a literary exercise, but also as a spiritual exercise, as an opportunity to encounter our souls anew. By attuning our souls to beauty, in all its complexity and brokenness, we might discover we have new songs to sing.

Note

1 Marilynne Robinson, *Reading Genesis* (New York: Farrar, Straus & Giroux, 2024), 21.

1

Soul Matters

I have come to think that care of the soul requires a high degree of resistance to the culture around us, simply because that culture is dedicated to values that have no concern for the soul.

—Thomas Merton, *Conjectures of a Guilty Bystander*

"What *is* the soul?"[1] If you are reading these words and you are not AI, I have some good news: *you* are a soul. But what does that mean and why does it matter in this increasingly secular age? In this chapter, we explore Robinson's tender and tenacious notion of the soul in her nonfiction, particularly her essays, which will provide the theoretical infrastructure for our later analysis of the beauty of souls in her fiction. Robinson refers to the soul as "the masterpiece of creation" that has been denied, defaced, and denigrated in modern reductionistic discourses.[2] Like any masterpiece, it merits serious examination, but our truncated anthropologies have blinded us to its beauty. Robinson wants to reaffirm and reclaim the soul in a culture that excludes and expunges it. She wants to celebrate the soul for its brilliance, untold contributions to culture and civilization, and inherent worth, value, and dignity. While waxing eloquent about the soul, she always leaves room for mystery, asserting that we will never plumb the depths of our "extensionless and undiscoverable souls."[3] And yet, souls continually surface like the tip of icebergs that conceal much more than they reveal, ever floating in the ocean of being.

But *what* is a soul? Always elegant and elusive, Robinson refuses to give simple definitions for complex realities. Nevertheless, she crystallizes her theory of soul (or mind, or self, she uses these terms interchangeably depending on the context) throughout her nonfiction, particularly in polemical engagement with modern reductionistic characterizations of the self as simply the product of sexual impulses (Freudianism), economic forces (Marxism), or blind biology (materialism).[4] All these explain human nature as reducible to something else, which ultimately explains it away. "The real assertion being made in all this," Robinson declares, contemptuously, "is that there is no soul."[5] No soul? You can almost hear the indignation in her literary voice. How could beings who have created literature, music, painting, architecture, these monuments to culture, define themselves out of existence? How can they deny the miracle of their reality, with its beauty and delicate intricacies? How could we witness the breakthroughs in science and technology only to dismiss ourselves as fabrications? What has happened?

Something has gone terribly wrong in contemporary estimations of the human person. Theology and philosophy have been supplanted by ideology, in her view, an ideology that overreaches beyond its methods. "Modern discourse is not really comfortable with the word 'soul,' and in my opinion the loss of the word has been disabling, not only to religion but to literature and political thought and to every humane pursuit."[6] Too many in the intelligentsia and scientific community uncritically assent to these simplistic and totalizing discourses to the detriment of human flourishing in art, culture, politics, religion, and any other edifice to the human overplus of being and meaning. Against the "closed circle that is called modern thought," Robinson unapologetically posits the reality of a soul, including her own.[7] Against their reductionism and "dreary determinisms," she seeks to expand the self, to let it soar to new heights.[8] She never tires of identifying the mind as the most complex reality in the universe.[9]

When invoking the term *soul*, she signifies the exceptionality and dignity of her subject contra the trivialization of today's flattened anthropologies: "The word *soul* authorizes a scale and seriousness in the conception of the human being that has no equivalent when the subject is broached in other terms."[10] As we will see, it acknowledges the "absolute dignity and significance" of every person, as well as affirming the cosmic meaningfulness of their existence.[11] She also affirms the immortality of the soul, its continuation after death, without diminishing the value of its daily mortal existence.[12] John Flavel, the English Puritan, expresses the dignity of the soul in *A Treatise of the Soul of Man*, which Robinson quotes approvingly: "The soul is the most wonderful and astonishing piece of divine workmanship; it is no hyperbole to call it the breath of God, the beauty of men, the wonder of angels, and the envy of devils. One soul is of more value than all the bodies in the world."[13] In other words, the term *soul* signifies both its divine origin and its inherent dignity and value. But, still, what *exactly* is a soul?

A soul, for Robinson, is the center of consciousness, relationship, activity, and possibility that constitutes the human person in their irreducible uniqueness within a shared humanity. It is the "nexus of the self" arising from the mind that is "so uniquely elegant and capable" that it "merits a name that would indicate a difference in kind from the ontological run of things, and for my purposes 'soul' would do nicely."[14] She alternates between "mind" or "soul," never quite providing a precise definition, operating provisionally and tentatively ("for my purposes"). This is not an oversight or philosophical sloppiness. An explicit, exhaustive definition of the soul would claim mastery over and thus dispel the mystery of inwardness.[15] When it comes to core concepts, Robinson opts for obliqueness over direct definition. Naturally, she identifies her subject, but she frequently talks around it to give it shape, rather than starting with an authoritative definition or assumption. Experience guides her engagement with reality, especially the reality of souls: "The advice I give my students is the advice I give myself—forget definition, forget assumption, watch."[16]

And she has followed her own advice. She has peered deeply inward and discovered vast caverns. She has gazed outward to discover a world of souls in endlessly complex relationships. From these wells of experience, she will venture preliminary definitions of the soul/mind/self: "The mind, whatever else it is, is a constant of everyone's experience, and, in more and other ways than we know, the creator of the reality that we live within, that we live by and for and despite, and that, often enough, we die from. Nothing is more essential to us."[17] Note first that here, in one of her more robust definitions, she respects the mystery of the mind, its surplus of reality and meaning. Beyond these conceptual contours, there is always more than we can grasp or express. "Whatever else it is" signals the horizon of the mind's mystery that she acknowledges at the outset. Next, she notes its experiential constancy—we are always with our mind, in it, to employ a spatial metaphor—wherein all perceptions, receptions, actions, and expressions sync to our continual, pre-theoretical sense of self as the subject of these vast and varied experiences.

Gesturing once again to mystery—"in more and other ways than we know"—she sees the mind as our reality-generator, the source of the constructions of reality we inhabit. As such, it is fundamental to our moment-to-moment experience: "Nothing is more essential to us."[18] Whenever exploring the fundamentals of human existence, Robinson exercises caution, restraining herself from conceptual finality. Contemporary stories of the self that reduce them to some known quality (sex, economy, biology) trample on the mystery and thereby distort their elusive and complex reality, which defies simple frameworks that bracket the surplus of meaning of the self. Robinson sees the self as infinitely intricate, and yet there are things we can know and say about it. On the one hand, we know it more than anything else; on the other hand, it remains forever remote. Like the horizon, it recedes the closer we get to it because we exist inside of it and in relation to it as we navigate existence.

As souls, that is, as self-conscious selves, we exist in relation to our own thoughts, experiences, and aspirations: "Then there is the odd privilege of existence as a coherent self, the ability to speak the word 'I' and mean by it a richly individual history of experience, perception, and thought."[19] In an interview, Robinson shares how teachers impressed upon her the centrality of this relationship of self to self: "We were positively encouraged to create for ourselves minds we would want to live with. I had teachers articulate that to me: 'You have to live with your mind your whole life.' You build your mind, so make it into something you want to live with. Nobody has ever said anything more valuable to me."[20] There is no place to hide from yourself: the soul accompanies you in every conscious and subconscious moment. Hence, life as a soul entails a continual, dynamic, evolving relationship of the self with the self. Like any relationship, it takes work. Since the self is the self's principal relationship, it stands to reason it ought to take priority. Failure to build, renovate, and adorn the mind renders it psychologically and emotionally inhospitable. Only once we have acknowledged the primary relationship of the self with the self, and understood its experiential primacy, can we begin the lifelong work of soul-formation.

The eye of the soul does not only turn inward, constructing its own inner cathedrals, oblivious to the outside world in its monadic mania. It also turns outward, looking for souls with whom it can share its unearthed treasure. Interpersonally, the soul's outwarding involves traversing the intellectual, experiential, and emotional space between the self and others, a dominant theme in Robinson's fiction. Artistically, it involves manifesting a vision of beauty in concrete art forms: "Each of us lives intensely within herself or himself, continuously assimilating past and present experience to a narrative and vision that are unique in every case yet profoundly communicable, whence the arts."[21] In every relationship our souls bridge solitudes. In every artistic experience the soul of the artist speaks to the soul of the witness. Souls seek encounter with other souls, ways to share their solitude, through shared experiences and understanding. Interpersonal relationships are ultimately soul connections.

Why should we embrace the concept of the soul? Robinson would return to her empirical epistemology: look, see, interpret. In her view, the soul has obvious heuristic value: "I find the soul a valuable concept, a statement of the dignity of a human life and of the unutterable gravity of human action and experience."[22] Soul, as an idea, helps to explain life, culture, and reality better than the ideological alternatives she rails against in her nonfiction. It is a helpful notion because it gestures toward the soul's impact on the world, which has been formative and deformative: "As proof of the existence of mind we have only history and civilization, art, science, and philosophy."[23] No other creature, no other force of nature, has transformed the globe like the mind. In a mic-drop indictment, Robinson points out the obvious truth that contemporary reductionistic frameworks obscure or obviate: "Human consciousness has at least as great an impact on the planet as any force of nature, yet its existence is in doubt because science does not know how to describe it."[24]

In her theological gloss of the story of the tower of Babel, she underscores the grandeur of humanity, with its godlike capacities: "Now that we have split the atom and sliced the gene and sent a kind of emissary into interstellar space we have some idea of the possibilities the Lord saw adumbrated in the aspirations of humankind."[25] God disperses precocious humanity from Babel perhaps to avoid or forestall the catastrophes humanity invariably unleashes with its technical prowess: "If God had dispersed the collaborators who made up the Manhattan Projects, or any analogous project, this earth might be better for it, or at least viable in the longer term."[26] This "overplus of human ability"[27] inspires awe in Robinson, the sense that as a species, as souls in the collective, we have a godlike power over the planet: "Every day we are confronted with the actual and potential effects of this power, but we are never properly in awe of it."[28] Who can deny souls when their impact is so profound? Only those who preclude it as a fundamental presupposition to their new narrative.

At an abstract level, Robinson finds the concept of the soul interesting. At a concrete level, she finds *herself* interesting: "I would add that I find my own soul interesting company, if this did not seem to cast doubt on my impeccable objectivity. This is not entirely a joke."[29] Robinson illustrates her notion of soul expression through the process of writing fiction. Where do her characters come from? What purpose does fiction serve? These questions, she says, are unanswerable.[30] They are part of the depths of the soul's creativity. Writing, at least for her, "consists very largely of exploring intuition."[31] She does not hatch an intricate plot that plays out through the conventional means of event-driven, thrill-seeking storytelling. Any reader of her fiction will nod knowingly. For her, fiction creation involves the discovery of a voice or a picture that she slowly comes to know more intimately over time: "A character is really the sense of a character, embodied, attired, and given voice as he or she seems to require."[32] Her stories, then, unfold through dawning intuition rather than the prior architectonics of world-building or narrative construction. As she gets to know her characters better, she puts them in situations that make sense, and a story begins to materialize.

Every so often, Robinson gives us a window into her soul, which illuminates her theory of souls: what they are and what they do. She would have been a poet, she says, but became instead a fiction writer.[33] Writing, for her, consists of forays into the "frontiers of the unsayable": "[A]s a writer, I continuously attempt to make inroads on the vast terrain of what cannot be said—or said by me, at least. I seem to know by intuition a great deal that I cannot find words for, and to enlarge the field of my intuition every time I fail again to find these words."[34] Robinson intuitively knew she was a writer: "I remember once, as a child, walking into a library, looking around at the books, and thinking, I could do that."[35] For years she harbored that hidden knowledge until she finally externalized it: "In fact I didn't do it until well into my thirties, but the affinity I felt with books as such preserved in me the secret knowledge that I was a writer when any dispassionate appraisal of my life would have dismissed the notion entirely."[36] Souls, we learn from her experience as a writer, have talents and intuitions that await actualization. She was a writer in waiting before she wrote *Housekeeping*. Her poetic proclivities pervade her fiction, especially in *Jack*.

Contemporary anthropologies dehumanize the soul through reductionistic caricatures: "humankind as a naked ape, as phenotype of the selfish gene."[37] They level the person to a state, function, or mode of being, which has enormous ethical consequences. Instead of affirming the inherent beauty, value, and dignity of souls, we can dismiss them as part of a faceless category. Instead of eliciting their hidden potential, we can slot them into prescribed societal roles until their inner genius lies so deeply buried it becomes totally inaccessible. Once we reduce the soul to a type, a person to a process, a name to a number, there is no limit to the ways we can infringe on their rights and deface their dignity. Human history furnishes us with a ready array of examples of our capacity to dehumanize and instrumentalize systematically, and of our endless ability to justify every cruelty, violation, and exploitation as necessary and even praiseworthy.

Not so when we treat them as a soul: "The word *soul* . . . uniquely invests each individual person with an absolute dignity and significance."[38] The moment we recognize in the other a spark of divinity with limitless possibilities, in complicated relationships, with dreams as real and vivid and valued as our own, we can no longer treat them as *merely* instantiations of types or objects of study or resources to manage. Robinson frames her interpersonal ethics in terms of soul-to-soul relation: "We do not deal with one another as soul to soul . . ."[39] When we see other souls as akin to our own, fumbling and searching for their way like us, we can no longer dismiss them as generic, irrelevant, or disposable. We study the recesses of deep space with awe and wonder but fail to see the marvels before us every day: "If we are to consider the heavens, how much more are we to consider the magnificent energies of consciousness that make whomever we pass on the street a far grander marvel than our galaxy?"[40]

It is a lofty goal, to treat each other as soul to soul. It would require, if taken to heart, extreme attentiveness, consideration, and grace. In fact, it would immobilize social interactions, if taken too far. How do we make small talk with a soul, given its exalted position in the cosmos? It would seem impertinent, even sacrilegious, considering its sacred status. How do we discuss the minutiae of employment, the logistics of a transaction, the strategies for a game, or simply wave across the street? Souls, the crown jewels of creation, deserve and even demand so much more. In short, it is overwhelming and unsustainable, which she signals; "So many voices, so many worlds, we can weary of them."[41] Sometimes we must remain in the shallows of existence with other souls. It requires careful discernment and deliberation to know how deep to go in our interpersonal interactions: we cannot enter the depths with every soul we meet. We would drown. Not every encounter can be soul to soul, but every interaction between souls can be underwritten with respect and acknowledgment. Even in mundane exchanges, soul subscripts operate, hallowing every encounter at a subterranean level that always contains the possibility of surfacing.

"Science tells us we have no souls."[42] Every instinct in Robinson rails against that hasty conclusion. Whence our sense of self as more than biologically coded, more than societally shaped, more than merely economically driven? Whence our companionship and conflict with our own thoughts, dreams, and memories? Whence our capacity for science, art, and culture? Whence the emotional and spiritual truth behind the old hymn "It Is Well with My Soul"? These inward experiences, albeit elusive and resistant to empirical analysis, cannot be so easily swept away. She jokes: "No song says, 'It is well with my superego.'"[43] No, when science outstrips its methods, it becomes just another dogmatism, "scientism" instead of scientific. Our experience displays the beauty and brilliance of the soul too clearly for any specious theory to deny it credibly. No soul? Nonsense. We radiate soul.

Robinson's theory of souls underpins her fiction, animating her characters with a deep spirituality, even those who struggle with and reject religion, perhaps especially so. In her novels, the spiritual verisimilitude of her most beloved characters pierces through the pages as they celebrate beauty, relate to their environment, and come to terms with their life. Robinson shapes each of them with an indelible quality of soul, including a history, context, and experiences, as well as clearly definable characteristics and sensibilities that constitute their fictional identity. She crafts them with care, attends to them with tenderness, and then, half-regretfully puts them in interesting narrative situations. As readers, we become attached to them, invested in their stories, moved by their relationships, and hopeful for their flourishing in fictional futures we never see. In short, we develop a reader-relationship with them where their fictional "souls" shape and transform our nonfictional souls.[44] In this encounter we have a heightened awareness of ourselves as souls in need of crafting, attention, and expression. The manifold spiritual implications of the dawning awareness of ourselves as souls shining in our distinctive environments will occupy us for the rest of the chapter.

Soulful living requires, firstly, the recognition of ourselves as souls. The famous Delphic injunction—know thyself—echoes through the centuries, whispering to souls to awaken to their own reality and to embark on a journey of self-discovery, which takes the self into its inner recesses, where it enters vast unexplored caverns glittering with treasures. Once we see ourselves as souls—as a distinctive center of consciousness arising from a particular biological, social, and historical context with unique experiential histories—we can start on the road toward a more fully realized spiritual life, where we let our souls shine more fully. Those who deny the soul, who dismiss the self as illusory or epiphenomenal or insignificant, reject the spiritual journey at the outset. They hide the soul's light. Spiritual vitality begins with the knowledge of the self as a soul, as a being beyond its impulses and functionalities.

Robinson continually affirms the soul as wonderful and precious. She grounds her appraisal theologically and experientially. Souls are created and loved by God, which confers inestimable value: "the divine likenesses among whom we live are of the highest interest and value to God . . . anyone we encounter is an image of God."[45] The tradition of the *imago Dei*—humans created in the image of God—underwrites her theological anthropology: "Then God said, 'Let us make humankind in our image, according to our likeness. . . . So God created humankind in his image, in the image of God he created them; male and female he created them" (Genesis 1:26–27).[46] She also extols the soul's productions, from the macro level of culture and civilization to the micro level of art, science, and politics. She considers the collective history of souls, saying, in effect, look, see what we are capable of, see all the wonders of the world we have created.[47] Look also at our capacity for destruction: environmentally, socially, politically, and interpersonally. Her early book *Mother Country* explores an urgent and alarming aspect of that dark capacity.[48]

Once we recognize and affirm our status and value as souls created in the image of God, we face the reality of freedom. Souls are free. They are not totally free with an unfettered, unlimited, unconditioned agency that permits any possibility. Absolute freedom belongs to God alone as a prerogative of divine omnipotence and aseity. No, human freedom faces all sorts of constraints: historical, social, economic, educational, physical, psychological, practical, and many others. And yet, even amid the myriad of mitigating factors, we are free to make meaningful choices: marriage, children, friends, employment, hobbies, and many others. Freedom signifies the power to shape our souls in significant ways, to follow our interests, to actualize our potential, to make our mark on the world. Certainly, we are not free to the same degree; some have greater privileges and opportunities, some face more obstacles than others and must work twice as hard for half the result, both now and in the past. But in all ages humans have been free to shape their souls.

Freedom places a heavy moral burden on the soul. It comes with many responsibilities. Robinson sees the care of the soul as a sacred obligation, given its divine status, vast potential, irreplaceable uniqueness, and eternal destiny. Moreover, it is an obligation that cannot be delegated: no one else can exist in the world as we exist, no one can perceive as we perceive, or can give what we can give.[49] The urge to shift responsibility to another or to blame someone else when things go awry has ancient origins. Look no further than the story of the fall of humanity in Genesis 3. After they disobey the prelapsarian prohibition against eating from the tree of the knowledge of good and evil, Adam blames Eve for the initial violation, and she, in turn, blames the serpent, who presumably (if we adopt the Luciferian psychology of *Paradise Lost*) blames God. They all abdicate personal responsibility in favor of a victim mentality, to their own physical and spiritual detriment. No, to be a soul is to make choices and to accept the consequences of those choices.

But consequences are not always evenly meted out. The good suffer, the bad prosper, and injustices exist around every corner. Ancient Job teaches us the painful misalignment between good and evil and reward and punishment. It does not always level out, and sometimes the scales tip unfairly, and sometimes they smash altogether. So while freedom implies responsibility, including consequences, it also exposes a mystery about the inequity of reality. Life is not fair. Good does not always triumph in this world. The problem of evil remains a mystery, a very troubling mystery, that calls for wisdom and compassion. Robinson raises the problem of evil several times in her nonfiction.[50] She does not attempt to solve it but to "let it stand" insistent and yet unanswered.[51] It relates to freedom surely, but she does not subscribe to the classic free-will defense because it simplifies knotty realities.

The realization of the complexity of the soul's employment of freedom, with its attendant pressures and unforeseen outcomes, calls for grace. Grace is a major theme in Robinson's nonfiction as well.[52] Once again, with theological and philosophical concepts, Robinson takes a tentative approach: "What *is* grace, after all?"[53] Metaphysics requires measure, reserve, and room for mystery. Grace arises from the rubble of ruin: lies, failures, betrayals. It is the effect of love in a fallen world. What is grace? "Grace is grace," she echoes from William Shakespeare's *Measure for Measure*.[54] Tautology here serves not to evade the question but to point to the answer: see, experience, discover. "'Grace is grace'—simply itself, not accessible to paraphrase."[55] Its unparaphrasability does not entail its total incomprehensibility, however. It is the gratuitous, unmerited, unexpected, unasked, unconditional extension of forgiveness.[56] In other words, it is love in the context of wrongs, wrongs that demand either punishment or pardon. Grace emerges as a motif in Robinson's fiction when characters misuse their freedom to harm others.

For Robinson, souls have a moral imperative to care for other souls, not harm them. Her soul-to-soul injunction constitutes a theological ethics grounded in her theological anthropology: "We can be so contemptuous and abusive of one another, we images of God who are so prone to desecrating other images of God, individually and collectively."[57] All souls have been created by God, all have hopes and dreams, all have untapped potential, so all deserve respect. Violence, exploitation, prejudice, marginalization, neglect, disenfranchisement, and all other forms of soul-to-soul damage violate the fundamental spiritual kinship between souls, deny or denigrate their inherent value and dignity, and efface one's own soul, which becomes tainted in the process.[58] Robinson's ethics, particularly her interpersonal ethics, have as their clarion call the recognition and affirmation of the beauty of other souls toward whom we also have unshirkable responsibilities.[59]

Applied socially, it entails developing structures, programs, and policies that enable souls to flourish. Robinson identifies as a classic liberal, a designation that signifies open-handedness to the neighbor. She wholeheartedly embraces liberal generosity: "I attach religious value to generous, need I say liberal, social policy. . . . The word 'liberal' has been effectively stigmatized. . . . As if generosity were culpable."[60] But she does not shy away from the designation: "I am myself liberal. By that I mean society exists to nurture and liberate the human spirit, and that large-mindedness and openhandedness are the means by which these things are to be accomplished."[61] As with all her great loves—Christianity, America, the academy—she critiques liberalism's failure to live up to its ideals: "I am very critical of liberalism, not in principle but as a movement. . . . As a principle, liberalism is essential to the sanity and humanity of this civilization. As a movement, it is virtually defunct."[62] Since souls live in society, society ought to provide a humane and hospitable environment, which it consistently fails to do, she bemoans.

Applied politically, her soul-to-soul ethics precludes polemics. Naturally, different political parties of divergent ideological persuasions ought to engage in vigorous debate, but when the debate devolves into personal attacks and the castigation of entire voting blocks, the opponent's soul becomes overshadowed by animus. Ironically, and perhaps instructively, Robinson seems to have fallen prey to polemics when her aging mother became engrossed in and agitated by Fox News in her final years. The endless stream of anger and alarmism infiltrated her consciousness, engendering needless worry and confusion. Even worse, it caused her to turn against her own daughter, despite her success and deep faith. Robinson's prose is fraught with restrained emotion: "I, her daughter, a self-professed liberal, was one of those who had ruined America. I would go to hell for it, too, a fact she considered both regrettable and just."[63] The flood dams break, however, when she directs her hurt and hostility toward one of the Fox News hosts who hijacked her mother's mind and emotions in her frailty: "I saw a clip of some Fox blondie saying that our conversation proved that Obama hated Christianity. . . . I know that the impassioned little commentator might actually have found a way to believe what she said."[64]

Obviously this is very uncharacteristic of Robinson. Dismissive slights do not become her. It goes against her general posture of grace and her calls for treating each other soul to soul. She quickly corrects course: "One mother, one life to live . . . I wish it could have ended better for both of us."[65] Of course we should extend her grace for this lapse, understandable given the heightened emotional context, but it demonstrates the difficulty of living soul to soul when politics intrude and devolve into polemics. We are all susceptible to the dehumanizing distortions that overtake combatants on both sides of the political divide. We hurl invectives at the other side with a sense of self-righteous impunity, forgetting they are souls, ignoring the validity first of their point of view and eventually of their right to have it. It only gets worse from there if left unchecked, so the soul-to-soul ethic must never be jettisoned in the heat of political battle, especially when it becomes personal, as it did for Robinson vis-à-vis Fox News. The primal instinct to name the other "an enemy" and then to turn on them viciously runs too deep. It must be vigilantly guarded against.

Robinson's unwavering defense of the soul against various modern denials need not alienate atheists or agnostics, whose numbers are on the rise.[66] Neither the denial of God's existence (atheism) nor uncertainty about it (agnosticism) necessarily negates the notion of a soul. For the atheist, the soul could simply signify the essential self, the self-consciousness that is tied to the life of the brain, and ceases afterwards, or continues only figuratively in its contribution through its soul-stamp on other people, ideas, or culture. For the agnostic, it could also denote the self whose origin and destiny remain unknown. For both, the concept of the soul could reinscribe the meaningfulness of terrestrial life, even in the absence of the divine. Even secular cosmologies and anthropologies can affirm the value of the spark of consciousness that flickers briefly before being extinguished, especially since it only takes a spark to ignite humanistic transformations of society. Robinson's implicit spirituality, which I will detail in the subsequent chapters, can easily be transposed into secular keys.

Similarly, her affirmation and celebration of souls translates into different world religions. In fact, it is inherently pluralistic, given her Christian universalism. As a Christian, she places Christ as "the origin and source of Being" and salvation. As a pluralist, she believes other faiths have access to the same cosmic creator and savior under different names. As a universalist, she believes all souls will be saved, that is, will experience postmortem consciousness and bliss: "This is my devoutest hope, not least because it promises our salvation, too."[67] She will entertain and dismiss some of the standard objections: "If salvation is universal, what about Hitler, Stalin? Well, hard cases make bad law."[68] Once you start with the exceptional cases, it is a slippery slope into the gates of hell, and it contracts her notion of grace, which she refuses to do: "The cost would be too high."[69] Robinson's religious sensibilities, while shaped by her Christian faith, remain open to other world religions, hence the versatility of her concept of soul.

Conclusion

Thus far, I have argued that Robinson develops a partial theory of souls in her nonfiction, which she demonstrates in her fiction at subtextual levels. Robinson's oblique theorization of the soul reflects her respect for the mystery and inaccessibility of metaphysical realities: soul, beauty, grace, and so on. To define them explicitly would presume mastery over realities that outstrip our noetic capacities, that are known through experiential encounters. Nonetheless, she affirms the soul's existence, vitality, and value contra reductionistic anthropologies that deny it in their instrumentalist accounts of humanity. I have traced the spiritual implications of her concept of the soul, which positions us to explore the spiritual insights of her fiction. Before that, in the next framing chapter, I will expand the argument beyond the mere reality of the soul to its capacity to create and apprehend beauty, which completes the main thesis of the study that Robinson's writings celebrate the beauty of souls and contain a latent spirituality for us to discover.

Notes

1 Marilynne Robinson, *The Givenness of Things* (New York: Farrar, Straus & Giroux, 2015), 235.

2 Marilynne Robinson, *When I Was a Child I Read Books* (New York: Farrar, Straus & Giroux, 2012), 8.

3 Robinson, *Reading Genesis*, 139.

4 Marilynne Robinson, *Absence of Mind: The Dispelling of Inwardness from the Modern Myth of the Self* (New Haven, CT: Yale University Press, 2010), 22.

5 Robinson, *The Givenness of Things*, 8. "So imperious is the materialist approach to reality that it considers whatever it cannot capture by its methods as effectively nonexistent, for example, the human self, the human mind." Marilynne Robinson, *What Are We Doing Here?* (New York: Farrar, Straus & Giroux, 2018), 128.

6 Robinson, *When I Was a Child I Read Books*, 8.
7 Robinson, *Absence of Mind*, x.
8 Robinson, *When I Was a Child I Read Books*, 5.
9 Robinson, *Absence of Mind*, 72, 135; cf. *When I Was a Child I Read Books*, 144.
10 Robinson, *What Are We Doing Here?*, 212.
11 Robinson, *What Are We Doing Here?*, 212.
12 Robinson, *Reading Genesis*, 47. She touchingly mentions parenthetically that she shares and treasures the "Christian belief in life after death" (47).
13 Robinson, *What Are We Doing Here?*, 213.
14 Robinson, *When I Was a Child I Read Books*, 8.
15 Robinson, *Absence of Mind*, 10.
16 Robinson, *When I Was a Child I Read Books*, 7.
17 Robinson, *Absence of Mind*, 1.
18 Robinson, *Absence of Mind*, 1.
19 Robinson, *Absence of Mind*, 110.
20 Wyatt Mason, "The Revelations of Marilynne Robinson," *The New York Times Magazine*, October 1, 2014, https://www.nytimes.com/2014/10/05/magazine/the-revelations-of-marilynne-robinson.html.
21 Robinson, *Absence of Mind*, 132.
22 Robinson, *The Givenness of Things*, 9.
23 Robinson, *Absence of Mind*, 120.
24 Robinson, *What Are We Doing Here?*, 48.
25 Robinson, *Reading Genesis*, 73.
26 Robinson, *Reading Genesis*, 75.
27 Robinson, *Reading Genesis*, 75.
28 Robinson, *Reading Genesis*, 80.
29 Robinson, *The Givenness of Things*, 9.
30 Robinson, *When I Was a Child I Read Books*, 7.
31 Robinson, *When I Was a Child I Read Books*, 6.
32 Robinson, *When I Was a Child I Read Books*, 6.
33 Robinson, *When I Was a Child I Read Books*, 20, 28.
34 Robinson, *When I Was a Child I Read Books*, 20.
35 Robinson, *When I Was a Child I Read Books*, 22.
36 Robinson, *When I Was a Child I Read Books*, 22.
37 Robinson, *Reading Genesis*, 126. Robinson notes the contrast in the Bible: "Biblical anthropology begins with an exalted conception

of humanity, then ponders our errors and deficiencies and our capacities for grace and truth, within the world of meaningful freedom created for them by an omnipotent God." Robinson, *Reading Genesis*, 126–27.

38 Robinson, *What Are We Doing Here?*, 212.

39 Robinson, *When I Was a Child I Read Books*, 5.

40 Robinson, *When I Was a Child I Read Books*, 8.

41 Robinson, *The Givenness of Things*, 15.

42 Robinson, *What Are We Doing Here?*, 267.

43 Robinson, *What Are We Doing Here?*, 267.

44 To differentiate between fictional and nonfictional souls requires theological and philosophical nuance. Both "exist" insofar as they are "birthed" (imaginatively vs. bodily), have an inner life (derived vs. generated), relate to the world (narratively vs. interpersonally), and have their source in God (secondarily via the author vs. primarily via embodied existence). Their respective eternal destinies, if not a frivolous theological question, depend on their impact on nonfictional souls. Many readers will affirm their spiritual formation by Robinson's fiction, which gives Reverend John Ames an afterlife in a derivative, secondary sense. Fictional and nonfictional souls are not identical or merely souls in different ontological modes, especially since fictional souls cannot engage in reciprocal interpersonal relationships: they can speak to us and transform us, but not vice versa. In the end, from a spiritual standpoint, their value rests on how they inspire us to impact "real" or "actual" or "embodied" souls. The question of whether we live in a simulated reality merely adds another metaphysical layer to the question.

45 Robinson, *Reading Genesis*, 196–97.

46 Translation from *The New Oxford Annotated Bible: New Revised Standard Version with the Apocrypha*, ed. Michael D. Coogan, 5th ed. (Oxford: Oxford University Press, 2018), 12–13.

47 Robinson, *Reading Genesis*, 80.

48 Marilynne Robinson, *Mother Country: Britain, the Welfare State and Nuclear Pollution* (New York: Farrar, Straus & Giroux, 1989). Robinson, half-jokingly, acknowledges her "unheard-of cheek" in her critique of Britain's environmental policies as it relates to nuclear waste: "But we are talking about the world, after all, which history has placed in our most untrustworthy hands." Robinson,

Mother Country, 235. Significantly, she concludes her study by exhorting humanity to "consult with our souls" to preserve life. Robinson, *Mother Country*, 236.

49 "You are not in competition with anybody else. There's nobody else who can be you. Your uniqueness is guaranteed so long as you respect it." Marilynne Robinson, "An Interview with Marilynne Robinson," in *Balm in Gilead: A Theological Dialogue*, ed. Timothy Larsen and Keith L. Johnson (Downers Grove, IL: InterVarsity Press, 2019), 202.

50 Robinson, *When I Was a Child I Read Books*, 69; Robinson, *The Givenness of Things*, 214, 268; Robinson, *What Are We Doing Here?*, 37; Robinson, *Reading Genesis*, 3, 13–14, 17, 37–38, 103.

51 Robinson, *The Givenness of Things*, 214.

52 It is a theological preoccupation in her reading of Genesis: "I know of no other literature except certain late plays of Shakespeare that elevates grace as this book does." Robinson, *Reading Genesis*, 226.

53 Robinson, *The Givenness of Things*, 35.

54 Robinson, *The Givenness of Things*, 33.

55 Robinson, *The Givenness of Things*, 33.

56 Robinson, *The Givenness of Things*, 38–39.

57 Robinson, *Reading Genesis*, 43.

58 "We are disastrously erring and rebellious, and irreducibly sacred. And God is mindful of us." Robinson, *Reading Genesis*, 64–65.

59 She notes the mystery of the meaning of a single soul vis-à-vis the vast expanse of souls through the endless eons: "This moment [God's promise to Abraham to make him as numerous as the stars] addresses a great mystery—how is one unique life to be thought of over against God's intention that there should be, as there have been and are, uncountable multitudes of lives? Is the meaning of a single soul diminished by sheer numbers of souls? Do any of us exist in excess of God's capacity for awareness, compassion, or love?" Robinson, *Reading Genesis*, 97.

60 Robinson, *The Givenness of Things*, 94, 97.

61 Marilynne Robinson, *The Death of Adam: Essays on Modern Thought* (New York: Picador, 1998), 258.

62 Robinson, *The Death of Adam*, 259.

63 Robinson, *What Are We Doing Here?*, 298.

64 Robinson, *What Are We Doing Here?*, 299.

65 Robinson, *What Are We Doing Here?*, 299.
66 Michael Ruse, *Atheism: What Everyone Needs to Know* (Oxford: Oxford University Press, 2015), chap. 3.
67 Robinson, *The Givenness of Things*, 216.
68 Robinson, *The Givenness of Things*, 217.
69 Robinson, *The Givenness of Things*, 217.

2

Beauty Abounds

> What a piece of work is a man, how noble in reason, how infinite in faculty, in form and moving how express and admirable, in action how like an angel, in apprehension how like a god—the beauty of the world, the paragon of animals!
>
> —William Shakespeare, *Hamlet*

Beauty draws readers into Robinson's fiction. It suffuses the stories, characters, dialogue, and landscapes. In this chapter, we will explore Robinson's musings on beauty as a preparatory step to an analysis of her fiction through the spiritual lens of the beauty of souls. Like soul, beauty is conceptually elusive, resistant to easy or exhaustive definition. It exists as something perceived, experienced, and apprehended at a deep level, the level of soul. What does she say about beauty in her essays, how do we encounter beauty in a world beset by distractions, dreariness, and despair, and, as it relates to the purpose of the study, how does beauty open vistas of spiritual insight in her fiction? To answer this constellation of questions, I will begin by explicating her working theory of beauty, located mainly in two short essays, after which I will identify the salient sites of beauty that arise in her essays.

On April 7, 2016, Robinson gave a talk entitled "Grace and Beauty" for the Comparative Literature Lecture Series at Princeton University, which appears in her latest essay collection.[1] Her talks, while always profound, are rarely systematic or structured in a conventional sense, so, once again, we should not expect a simple and straightforward definition of beauty. Instead, we must weave together the different aesthetic strands that she lays out into a recognizable pattern. Early on, she states: "Beauty disciplines."[2] The universe unfolds in unfathomable galaxies, and the mind emerges from Being and reaches for it, shapes it, and seeks to understand it. How does beauty discipline? It creates from the chaos and complexity of being coherent realities that resonate with our aesthetic sensibilities.

She gives as an example the creation of fictional characters, her specialty: "Character implies consistency of a kind. A word, even a punctuation mark, can be out of character.

There is an inaudible equivalent of a clang or a clunk where this kind of mistake is made."[3] Writers, then, must know their characters intimately, *listen* to them, in a way, in order to avoid false notes and missteps. What is this process? It is "an aesthetic response," an ear for the right frequency, a testament to artistic credibility, in other words, a discipline.[4] Part of the discipline involves balancing character shape and freedom to surprise: "I am speaking only of my own sense that to have the feeling of human presence about him or her a character has to seem free and constrained simultaneously, and that when this ceases to be true, credibility is lost."[5] This rings true to experience: we talk about people acting "out of character," so it stands to reason that her fictional characters have an artistic horizon within which they maneuver and sometimes stray.

Beauty disciplines by coercing the writer to give the character an authentic artistic aura: "Practically speaking, when I am writing I tend to think of a character as having a palette or a music. An aesthetic, in other words."[6] Limitation and variation, constraint and freedom, all balanced within an aesthetic particular to the character bring it to life. Robinson clarifies that her process does not begin with these principles but rather with "a sense of the experience of a human presence."[7] Through sustained introspection on that interior presence she develops her aesthetic atmospherics for a place and aura for a person, which creates a new space in the universe for being. Now, Robinson seems to be straying from her subject in the explication of her writing process, as she jokes: "What all this has to do with grace or beauty is not obvious at this point, I know."[8] Always oblique with metaphysics, we have come to expect her indirect approach, but she has laid the groundwork for a few principles.

Fiction writing, she continues, compels the writer to make decisions based on his or her knowledge of the characters. The author knows the characters intimately, not just things about them, and from that knowledge enjoys the liberation of aesthetic constraint: "As fiction develops, a writer has the exhilarating experience of losing options, of saying 'Of course!' to things that emerge on the page with an aura of necessity about them."[9] The choices of the author are "disciplined" by the constraints of the character, who then takes on a life of his or her own within the aesthetic confines of its fictional being, its aesthetic identity. Robinson grants them autonomy after creating or, better, discovering them. Ironically, what happens in the story can surprise her. Grace and beauty flows from the completion of the character from the initial inspiration to its emergent fictional reality, which transcends the author's original specifications. She repeatedly invokes the term *entelechy* to signify "the active principle of wholeness or completion in an individual thing," that is, applied to art, its dynamic artistic integrity and vitality.[10] Her characters have a recognizable identity, a wholeness.

Art, when done well, remains faithful to the inner experiences that generate it. Robinson reiterates in the essay that she wishes to "reauthorize the testimony of experience."[11] In her case, she had an experience of a voice, and her attentiveness to that experience brought something new to reality: "[T]he world would certainly never have felt the lack of an imaginary minister dying in Iowa in 1956 had anything intervened to stop me from writing a book. I would have felt no need to give an old man imagined life, and death, if I had not realized one afternoon that there was a highly particular voice in my head."[12] Introspection, realization, actualization. These are the products of the experience of the mind at work in ways that elude simple explanations. Where did the voice come from? She does not say because she does not know. Her mind, while hers, remains in a mysterious way independent of her, concealing depths she has yet to discover.

"So, beauty disciplines."[13] Circuitously, but with many fascinating observations, she returns to her point about beauty. Beauty involves attentiveness, selection, limitation, and apt expression: "It recommends a best word in a best place and makes the difference palpable between aesthetic right and wrong."[14] Beauty encounters the vast array of unfolding reality and makes choices about how to engage it and then how to present it: this subject, this structure, this mode of communication, down to the finest details. If it does not bring order to chaos per se, it at least spotlights an aspect of existence that illuminates reality, sometimes in a new or particularly lucid way. A poem can bring us to tears as it unearths our feelings of loss or delight. A song can lift the spirits as it activates euphoric feelings of community and gaiety. A novel about "an imaginary minister dying in Iowa in 1956" can shape our sense of the spiritual life.[15] Countless readers of Robinson would no doubt testify, yes and amen.

Beauty, as it balances between limitation and freedom, uncovers new terrain. It is inherently generative: "Beauty is like language in this. It can push at the borders of intelligibility and create new eloquence as it does so."[16] It is an "active principle," full of fecundity once the artist discovers his or her unique artistic vision.[17] Beauty "manifests" in reality, it breaks through, sometimes by accident, sometimes by careful design.[18] We have to follow our intuitions, trust our feelings, and let it flow through us in organic, authentic ways, never shortcutting the process for any expediency. She then, after waxing poetic about beauty, graces us with a concise definition of it: "the elegance of meaningful complexity."[19] Meaning*less* complexity is chaotic, inelegant, and disorientating. Meaning*ful* complexity—disciplined attentiveness to and actualization of the aspects of reality available and accessible to us—is orderly, elegant, and orientating. In a word, beautiful.

On April 15, 2015, Robinson delivered a lecture for the Veritas forum at Northwestern University entitled: "The Beautiful Changes."[20] In a few short paragraphs, she articulates a brief philosophy and theology of beauty. Both intimate rather than explicate, but they work in tandem to bring her theory of beauty into greater focus. The title derives from a poem that she cites at the outset: "One wading a Fall meadow finds on all sides / The Queen Anne's Lace lying like lilies / On water . . .—Richard Wilbur, 'The Beautiful Changes.'"[21] The poetic invocation sets the tone for the essay, a meditation on our perception of earthly beauty in its wider cosmic context. What is the world? It is, for her, the site of divine freedom and courtesy, the latter expressed in the fine-tuning of the cosmos, the former in God's ability to contravene natural laws.[22]

Thus begins her theology of beauty. God creates the cosmos with intention. God creates it as "an act of divine restraint, a covenant made with earthly life that put self-imposed limits on power that would otherwise overwhelm us, would effectively annihilate us."[23] God's freedom provides protection, provision, and predictability, all of which enable human survival and even flourishing. She points out that reality could have taken on an infinite number of qualities that probably defy conceptualization. She posits a surplus of being and potentiality outside of the "structures of our experience," which opens new possibilities of exploration and discovery. Her theology of beauty here underscores divine intentionality and design, but gestures to the great mysteries beyond the knowable. What is beautiful, theologically speaking? God's "courtesy" in opening a space in the infinite expanses of possible spaces and times for humanity, for our emergence. Design, rather than merely an argument for God's existence, functions here as an argument for divine aesthetics underwriting reality. But, as usual, it is a little hazy and abstract.

Robinson does not apologize for her elusiveness because deep reality and theological abstractions "elude definition": from grace and beauty to time and light.[24] These fundamental constituents of reality simply outstrip our physics and metaphysics and they shift based on the perceiver. She does not leave us philosophically bereft, however. She gives us another working definition from which we can develop her theory of beauty: "Some part of a definition of beauty ought to be that it is an aspect of experience that can, and possibly should, compel attention and also reward it."[25] This is a good starting point: beauty calls out to us as something worthy of our attention—worth our time, in colloquial terms. Beauty commandeers our soul, so to speak, dazzling, enrapturing, and transporting it. Moreover, it confers spiritual benefits. Any contact with beauty enriches the soul, so we ignore it at the expense of our spiritual thriving. It is also experiential, that is, it is not a concept to control but an experience to encounter. It tethers us to the world as we begin to see our connection to and absorption in its pulchritudinous plenitude.

So far, so good. We have an incipient philosophy of beauty as experiential, worthy of attention, and repaying sustained exposure at a spiritual level. Open, attentive souls encounter it continually as they adjust their spiritual eyes to the wonders of the world around them. Well and good, necessary, but not sufficient. She continues probing: "Yet the idea of beauty varies from one perceiver to the next, one decade to the next, and from culture to culture."[26] Now we are making progress. Beauty is variable, subjective, and culturally specific. We should expect "varieties of beauty" and learn to cultivate our appreciation of them.[27] No Platonic pure forms here, no monopolies on beauty, just kaleidoscopic experiential encounters. The beautiful changes over time and space and from soul to soul, but its existence as the endless horizon wherein souls find their place in the world transcends space and time: "If existence were designed to engraft us into the world, to charm and engage us, what could be better suited to accomplishing this than beauty, with its inexhaustible openness to variation, with its frangible and circumstantial rules and limits, which enable invention and tantalize perception?"[28] Beauty is the gravity of the soul.

Returning once again to theology, Robinson links beauty to grace: "The theologian can say that beauty eludes definition because it expresses the grace of God."[29] Beauty expands indefinitely, for Robinson, reaching far beyond what any definition would permit. Unmerited, unasked for, and often unpredictable, beauty breaks into reality, sometimes when we least expect it, like a flower pushing through the snow. We will see this play out in her fiction continually. Beauty expresses the grace of God in its power to bind the broken, to inspire the listless, to comfort the bereaved, to recall the wayward, and so much more. It heals, elevates, expands, reframes, and reorients. The work of beauty is as variable as the needs it encounters and the types of receptivity it meets. Its pliability is endless.

Her hybrid philosophical-theological theory of beauty invites participation, not merely cogitation. It is not an idea to grasp; it is an experience to enjoy, appreciate, and contribute to through our immersion in the flow of life. Perhaps that is why she so studiously avoids concrete, hardened definitions. It would limit the possibilities available to us. Instead, she wants to put us in a posture of receptivity: "Beauty awaits our notice."[30] Will we notice it, or will we pass it by, averting our gaze as we occupy our time and attention with lesser things? Beauty is ubiquitous: "Beauty is grandly present in the architecture of the cosmos, minutely present in the structure of the atom, and yet we humans can seem capable of utter indifference to it."[31] Pervasiveness does not guarantee perception. Blindless to beauty comes in many forms: neglect, bitterness, obstinance, indifference, and all the other roadblocks to spiritual flourishing. Somehow, in our awareness of our deficiencies, beauty becomes heightened as something we continually discover as a grace, as a gift from Beauty.

In her recent book *Reading Genesis*, Robinson returns to many of the themes enunciated in these two essays on beauty. She affirms the "sacredness in existence" that theism presumes.[32] She delights in the description of God enjoying "an evening breeze, a walk in the garden," in other words, enjoying the beauty of creation *with* humanity.[33] With exegetical keenness, she teases out the "extremely elegant detail" of Genesis 2:9: "The beauty of the trees is noted before the fact that they yield food."[34] For Robinson, this easily overlooked detail contains deep insight about the nature of existence: "Two things are signified, that God as the creator of beauty intends it for us to see and enjoy, and that He gives us the gifts of apprehension this pleasure requires, which is nothing less than a sharing of His mind with us in this important particular."[35] God creates the beauty, grants us the capacity to apprehend it, and makes it an existential priority.

These two essays on beauty are quintessentially Robinsonian. They are suggestive, elegant, elusive, and oblique.

For philosophers of religion and philosophical theologians, who trade in precise definition and careful argumentation, her approach can be infuriating. What is beauty? How do we know it? Where does it come from? What are its implications? Robinson refuses categorical answers, simple definitions, or even sometimes thematic consistency. That is her prerogative. Deeply learned, and well versed in theology and philosophy, she nonetheless operates more poetically than noetically, sometimes leaving the reader bemused. But her minimalism does not imply a lack of competence or concern; quite the opposite: it makes crucial metaphysical points. Philosophically, she argues that beauty, like other fundamental realities, "confound[s] our categories" and is "mutable": variable from person to person, culture to culture.[36] Theologically, she argues that beauty expresses God's grace, a gift woven into the very fabric of reality. Beauty disciplines insofar as it narrows our focus to the particular and forces us to attend to it within the parameters of its identity and in its freedom to evolve. In both essays, through different modes of discussion and argumentation, Robinson reiterates the need for attentiveness, openness, enrichment, and particularity.

Her theory of beauty, to the extent that it forgoes formal definitions, steers us toward spiritual encounters rather than critical examination. Instead of applying her theory of beauty to her fiction, we will instead follow her experiential recommendation. What is beauty? Remember her advice to her students about discovering the essence of humanity and human characters—souls, in other words: dispense with definition and first principles, simply watch.[37] She does not leave us unaided, however. Even though she does not put forward a conventional definition of beauty, she does talk around it, giving us important clues. Beauty abounds. It is ubiquitous, overflowing. Beauty deserves—even demands—our attention, despite our tendency to ignore it in the frantic hustle and bustle of everyday life. Beauty is mutable, changing depending on the context. Beauty generates, bringing new forms of beauty into the world that evocatively reflect or illuminate it. Beauty transforms.

If her theory sketches the shape of beauty generally, the motifs of her essays plot the promising locations more specifically. As focal points, they enable us to see not only the emphasis on the beauty of souls in her fiction, but also the spiritual implications and applications. The underlying assumption, of course, is that her nonfictional theory and preoccupations will surface in her fiction, although not always in a linear fashion. Beauty is not found in specious philosophies and theologies of beauty, her essays suggest, but in rich experiential encounters with ourselves, others, and the world. In other words, we cannot know *what* beauty is until we see *where* it is and engage it meaningfully. So where should we look as we turn to her fiction in the rest of the study for inroads into beauty?

It will come as no surprise that Robinson loves books.[38] The love affair started early: "When I was a child I read books. My reading was not indiscriminate. I preferred books that were old and thick and hard. . . . Relevance was precisely not an issue for me."[39] She immersed herself in the Bible, a lifelong preoccupation. *Moby-Dick* claims her highest admiration, "after the Bible of course."[40] She read the classics early in life: Horace, Virgil, Cicero. She has also read the American transcendentalists and the moderns.[41] Some books and authors reappear in her essays. She is infamous for her love of John Calvin, out of fashion in many of today's literary and theological circles, and is nearly notorious for her love of the much-reviled Puritan authors, whose cultural characterizations border on caricature.[42] Not so for Robinson: she finds them open, elegant, even beautiful. Robinson never looks to cultural critics for guidance in her reading or writing. In fact, her unconventional instincts almost forbid it. The beauty of books resides in their perennial ability to cast light upon and sometimes reshape our perception of reality.[43]

Sensitivity to language, down to the word, characterizes Robinson's reading and writing. She likens language to music: "I tell my students, language is music. Written words are musical notation."[44] Frequently in her essays she will fixate on a particular word. "Lonesome" can plunge her into reveries about the American West.[45] "Entelechy" has occupied her thoughts "for years."[46] Years! With a Hemingwayesque obsession with the *bon mot*, she delights in the employment of the perfect word for the perfect occasion: "One of the pleasures of writing is that so often I know that there is in fact a word that is perfect for the use I want to put it to, and when I summon it it comes, though I might not have thought of it for years."[47] Words embed philosophical and theological meaning at a microscopic level, and with a little etymological and literary archeology you can identify key insights: "Grace is gratuitous. Etymologies are lovely things."[48] Words wrapped with nuanced significations, language laced with cultural valences and values, some now defunct, these concerns find their way into her fiction frequently.

The writing process, especially the discovery and development of a character, absorbs her. They arise as a voice or a picture that gradually comes into focus and captures her attention.[49] When one of these voices or images emerges, it can captivate her completely: "Sometimes I am so struck by an image or an idea that I cannot sleep nights."[50] This discovery of a character, a story, then develops as she gives the character its shape, which involves sustained attention to its thoughts and voice as they germinate in her mind. Rarely does she know how it will proceed, only the aesthetic atmospherics that surround it. It engrosses her: "I have spent literal years of my life lovingly absorbed in the thoughts and perceptions of—who knows it better than I?—people who do not exist."[51] Not literally, of course, but they exist in her mind in an ontologically mysterious way, and they exist in the hearts and minds of her devoted readers vividly, in a way that can reshape consciousness. In addition to reading, then, the act of writing itself becomes a manifestation of beauty.

Harvesting inward beauty comes at a cost, however. The more she attends to the voices and images within, the more the world outside of her mind recedes into the background: "Sometimes, when I have spent days in my study dreaming a world while the world itself shines outside my windows, forgetting to call my mother because one of my nonbeings has come up with a thought that interests me, I think, this is a very odd way to spend a life."[52] Odd, certainly. Days dreaming new worlds into being as the world turns outside, nights consumed by awestruck ruminations. To say, colloquially, that she lives in her head would be true, even an understatement, but incomplete. More fulsomely, her continual internalization of beauty through books, through experience, and through heightened attentiveness enables her to concentrate beauty within and then capture it in her stories. She has cultivated an aesthetic frequency that others who similarly strive for the beautiful recognize, all through a life absorbed in and transported by reading and writing. That aesthetic fine-tuning, however, often takes her outside of physical reality, and that has costs.

As a writer, her fiction, particularly *Housekeeping* and *Gilead*, has made an indelible literary impact. In the first phase of this study, we have focused on her nonfiction to gain a purchase on the spiritual impact of her fiction, which will endure well beyond these works' early success. I mean no disrespect when I venture to guess that she will not be remembered for her nonfiction. Her essays and scholarly writing, while instructive and interesting, do not have the magic touch of her fiction. They have their own integrity and make their own contributions, but, in the history of literature, they will ultimately end up as a literary footnote. They provide the theoretical and biographical background to the driving questions, concerns, and sensibilities that inform her fiction. They afford us a peek behind the curtain, but only a peek. Mystery surrounds the origin of creative genius: "Two questions I can't really answer about fiction are (1) where it comes from, and (2) why we need it."[53] No number of scientific advancements in brain-imaging or human psychology will dispel the mystery of the origin of art and its beauty. The mystery itself is part of the beauty, as her approving quotation of Albert Einstein illustrates: "The most beautiful thing we can experience is the mysterious. It is the source of all true art and science."[54]

Nature and landscapes infuse Robinson's fiction with an aesthetic backdrop worthy of attention. As a product of the American West (Idaho), she was exposed to stunning vistas. As a long-time resident of New England, she has enjoyed the landscapes of the East as well. She shares stories of herself as a child wandering in the woods alone, "feeling the solitude around me build like electricity and pass through my body with a jolt that made my hair prickle." Nature was simultaneously other, a place of discovery, and of inwardness: "I remember kneeling by a creek that spilled and pooled among rocks and fallen trees . . . and thinking, there is only one thing wrong here, which is my own presence, and that is the slightest imaginable intrusion—feeling that my solitude, my loneliness, made me almost acceptable in so sacred a place."[55] Homey descriptions of chasing barn cats and feeding chickens at her grandparents' ranch illustrate her remarkable sensitivity to landscapes and homesteads as clearings of civilization.[56]

Relatedly, Robinson celebrates the beauty of society, especially in its least developed forms: small towns, isolated houses in no-man's-land. Nature is beautiful, yes, but so is the attempt to form a society, to keep the forces of chaos at bay. At a macro level, that entails the benevolence of social programs. At a micro level, it entails the small gestures of kindness and consideration found in any home where love abides. Robinson sees housekeeping as sacramental, a visible sign of invisible grace: "At a certain level housekeeping is a regime of small kindnesses, which, taken together, make the world salubrious, savory, and warm. I think of the acts of comfort offered and received within a household as precisely sacramental."[57] Naturally, domesticity can degenerate into less spiritual forms, even into oppression, but her instinct about the ways small, seemingly insignificant human interactions fill life with grace pervades her fiction, particularly in *Housekeeping* and *Home.*

More specifically still, Robinson sees family life as an incubator of beauty, despite the inevitable tensions and conflicts.[58] David, her brother, holds a special place in her heart, as she expresses in the dedication of *When I Was a Child I Read Books*: "For my brother David Summers, first and best of my teachers."[59] He shares some of her artistic visions and values.[60] In talks she will humorously note that she has not mentioned her brother for whole minutes. She also talks about her grandparents with warmth and nostalgia.[61] When it comes to her mother, however, she shares both her admiration and the struggles familiar between mothers and daughters. "She had lived a very private, sheltered, small-town life, never employed, devoted to her flowers and her dogs. She was a sharp-minded woman, aware and proud of her intelligence to the end of her life."[62] From this description I dare say her mother bears a striking resemblance to Robinson herself: sharp, private, attentive to beauty. And yet, as with so many family relationships, there were tensions: "She was complicated, and my relationship with her was never easy, but it was interesting, which was probably better for me, all in all."[63] As we explore her fiction, daily family dynamics, with their loves, joys, sorrows, resentments, and idiosyncrasies, become a focal point of beauty.

We could multiply the sites of beauty that Robinson highlights in her essays but let us name just a few more—for instance, music. Nearly every major life moment is accompanied by music. Birthdays have their famous ditty. Weddings employ formal processional music and, later, familiar upbeat dance numbers ("YMCA!"). Sports stadiums play songs to unite and activate fans ("Sweet Caroline"). Funerals often have soaring hymns. Anthems begin events. Music stirs emotions, captures moods, motivates actions, unites groups, and enhances special moments. It does more than stimulate and decorate, it accesses and activates common soul currents. Music transports us because it translates the complexity of our emotions and experiences into lyrics and tunes that we recognize and respond to at a visceral level. Robinson, of course, loves music, and in keeping with her unconventional, "unhip" way, she uses hymns to illustrate this.[64] In her later years she discovered a love of "elderly and old American hymns": "They can move me so deeply that I have difficulty even speaking about them."[65] She gives "In the Garden" and "I Love to Tell the Story," two dusty, nearly forgotten hymns, as examples, and they both have a sublime, subjective, experiential quality that makes the appeal understandable, given her aesthetic. All this in an essay entitled "Wondrous Love": her favorite hymn.

On Thursday, April 5, 2018, Wheaton College hosted a two-day conference entitled "Balm in Gilead: A Theological Dialogue with Marilynne Robinson." Baritone Roberts Sims sang "Balm in Gilead" to open the conference.[66] Strikingly, composer Shawn Okpebholo adapted and arranged "Wondrous Love," which visibly moved her. She had to take a moment to "collect herself,"[67] not least because the music incorporated nearly lost "Negro spirituals."[68] Beauty begets beauty: one work of art elicits reactions that underwrite or inspire another. Music, particularly hymns, pervade Robinson's fiction, but the deeper point is that artistic expressions tend to be generative when received by aesthetically tuned hearts and minds.[69] Artists find beauty and inspiration in other forms of art. A poem can inspire a song. A story can inspire a film. A film can inspire a musical, and so on. Beauty is generative.

It goes without saying that Robinson is publicly and unapologetically religious:[70] "I defer to no one in my love of America and for Christianity. I have devoted my life to the study of both of them."[71] Specifically, she affiliates with mainline Protestant Christianity, typically known for education, social activism, and progressivism.[72] She grew up in Presbyterian circles.[73] She currently belongs to the Congregational United Church of Christ.[74] "I have spent most of my life in Presbyterian and Congregational churches," ecclesial environments that undoubtably shaped many of her aesthetic and intellectual sensibilities, especially her love of music and literature.[75] Moreover, she has an abiding interest in theology, particularly Calvinism, so we should not be surprised to find references to religion and theology throughout her fiction.[76] In fact, they permeate her Gilead series. Despite her love of Christianity, she frequently criticizes it when she thinks it has been co-opted, compromised, or corrupted by a "Christianism" that betrays its fundamental principles.[77]

Finally, beauty is embodied. In this moment, as you read these words, you have a body, and exist in an embodied state, even though you are far more than your body, if you subscribe to Robinson's theory of souls. You are probably sitting, feeling hungry or satiated, tired or alert, uncomfortable or comfortable, just as I am. As embodied souls, our experiences are physically mediated, even our dreams connect to our physiology in ways we do not fully understand. Robinson wistfully chides herself for forgetting her embodiment sometimes: "I wish I had experienced my earthly life more deeply. It is my fault that I didn't. I could have been a better scholar of Walt Whitman."[78] She can be overly hard on the things she loves, including, in all probability, herself. The point to underscore here at the end of this chapter is that beauty is experienced in embodied ways, including eating, sleeping, waking, embracing, lovemaking, crying, laughing, aging, and the endless ways we interact with and experience the world physically and empirically. We are embodied souls, and we must not abstract or spiritualize ourselves out of physical existence, which just denies reality. We are on this floating orb, standing on these feet, seeing through these eyes, feeling with these hands.

After identifying several salient sites of beauty from her essays, it would be apposite to conclude with the observation that, for Robinson, beauty appears in unexpected places. This principle follows from her theory of the ubiquity of beauty: it is found everywhere, for those with eyes and a desire to see. Explicating these various sites of beauty will help to focus our analysis of her fiction in the coming chapters, but they do not circumscribe the limits of beauty, nor negate its resistance to simple formulas or categories. Beauty abounds, everywhere, all the time, cascading in every moment in roaring confluences visible only to those willing to see, who are available, attentive, and open to its surprising manifestations. The readiness is all.

Conclusion

Robinson does not forward an explicit, exhaustive definition of beauty, but she does parse it enough for us to formulate a theory of beauty that can guide our discussion. Beauty resides inside and outside of the soul. It patiently awaits our discovery: it asks us to take notice, appreciate it, and sometimes invites us to expand it through new creations. Beauty takes forms that have inner consistency while allowing for variation, an interplay of limitation and freedom that makes room for growth. Souls, creators and purveyors of beauty, perceive and receive it differently, ensuring an endless variety of beauty and its mutability over time and space. Beauty, that elusive concept, binds us to existence and to each other: it has an existential adhesive effect. Its ubiquity sacralizes reality, imbuing it with worth and meaning, summoning a posture of discovery and gratitude. Several sites of beauty emerge in Robinson's essays as significant, but it can always appear in unexpected places. Like shells on the seashore, each has its own distinctive shape and hue, and sometimes beneath an inauspicious cover you find the most dazzling colors.

Notes

1 Robinson, *What Are We Doing Here?*, 101–14.
2 Robinson, *What Are We Doing Here?*, 101.
3 Robinson, *What Are We Doing Here?*, 104.
4 Robinson, *What Are We Doing Here?*, 104.
5 Robinson, *What Are We Doing Here?*, 104.
6 Robinson, *What Are We Doing Here?*, 104.
7 Robinson, *What Are We Doing Here?*, 105.
8 Robinson, *What Are We Doing Here?*, 106.
9 Robinson, *What Are We Doing Here?*, 106.
10 Robinson, *What Are We Doing Here?*, 106, 111, 113.
11 Robinson, *What Are We Doing Here?*, 109; cf. 103, 110.
12 Robinson, *What Are We Doing Here?*, 110.
13 Robinson, *What Are We Doing Here?*, 112.
14 Robinson, *What Are We Doing Here?*, 112.
15 Robinson, *What Are We Doing Here?*, 110.
16 Robinson, *What Are We Doing Here?*, 112.
17 Robinson, *What Are We Doing Here?*, 112.
18 Robinson, *What Are We Doing Here?*, 112.

19 Robinson, *What Are We Doing Here?*, 113. In another essay, she says "beauty is a strategy of emphasis," wherein we recognize the aspect of reality the author illuminates through special attention vis-à-vis the rest of reality. Robinson, *The Givenness of Things*, 111. Once again, these are partial definitions that we must weave together into a viable, if not philosophically and theologically comprehensive, theory of beauty.

20 Robinson, *What Are We Doing Here?*, 127–33.

21 Robinson, *What Are We Doing Here?*, 127. The poem compares the beauty of a flower-laden field to a lily-laden lake, so here the beautiful changes from terrestrial to aquatic or interprets the terrestrial through the aquatic.

22 Robinson, *What Are We Doing Here?*, 127.

23 Robinson, *What Are We Doing Here?*, 128.

24 Robinson, *What Are We Doing Here?*, 129.

25 Robinson, *What Are We Doing Here?*, 129.

26 Robinson, *What Are We Doing Here?*, 129.

27 Robinson, *What Are We Doing Here?*, 129.

28 Robinson, *What Are We Doing Here?*, 129.

29 Robinson, *What Are We Doing Here?*, 129.

30 Robinson, *What Are We Doing Here?*, 132.

31 Robinson, *What Are We Doing Here?*, 132.

32 Robinson, *Reading Genesis*, 26; cf. 71.

33 Robinson, *Reading Genesis*, 31.

34 Robinson, *Reading Genesis*, 39.

35 Robinson, *Reading Genesis*, 39.

36 Robinson, *What Are We Doing Here?*, 129.

37 Robinson, *When I Was a Child I Read Books*, 7.

38 "Open a book and a voice speaks. A world, more or less alien or welcoming, emerges to enrich a reader's store of hypotheses about how life is to be understood." Robinson, *The Givenness of Things*, 15.

39 Robinson, *When I Was a Child I Read Books*, 85. "My pleasures are the same—books and plays, church and teaching—and my feelings about them are changed only in degree." Robinson, *The Givenness of Things*, 217.

40 Thomas Schaub, "An Interview with Marilynne Robinson," *Contemporary Literature* 35 (1994): 234.

41 Robinson, *When I Was a Child I Read Books*, 86–87.

42 Robinson, *The Givenness of Things*, 116; *What Are We Doing Here?*, 136.

43 She gives an example from Jonathan Edwards, whose footnote on moonlight in *The Great Christian Doctrine of Original Sin Defended* transformed her "sense of reality." Robinson, *What Are We Doing Here?*, 51.

44 Robinson, *When I Was a Child I Read Books*, 130; cf. *The Givenness of Things*, 111.

45 Robinson, *When I Was a Child I Read Books*, 88–89.

46 Robinson, *What Are We Doing Here?*, 106.

47 Robinson, *When I Was a Child I Read Books*, 22.

48 Robinson, *The Givenness of Things*, 38.

49 Robinson, *The Givenness of Things*, 218.

50 Robinson, *The Givenness of Things*, 218.

51 Robinson, *When I Was a Child I Read Books*, 21.

52 Robinson, *When I Was a Child I Read Books*, 23.

53 Robinson, *When I Was a Child I Read Books*, 7; cf. *The Givenness of Things*, 111.

54 Robinson, *The Givenness of Things*, 151.

55 Robinson, *When I Was a Child I Read Books*, 88.

56 Robinson, *When I Was a Child I Read Books*, 88–89.

57 Robinson, *When I Was a Child I Read Books*, 93.

58 Robinson, *The Givenness of Things*, 281.

59 Robinson, *When I Was a Child I Read Books*, 5.

60 Robinson, *When I Was a Child I Read Books*, 86.

61 Robinson, *When I Was a Child I Read Books*, 88–89; Robinson, *The Death of Adam*, 235.

62 Robinson, *What Are We Doing Here?*, 297.

63 Robinson, *What Are We Doing Here?*, 297.

64 Refreshingly in today's image-conscious (obsessed?) world, she does not shy away from poking fun at herself: "Recently I read a brief overview of myself and my work, an article on the Internet. It said that if someone were bioengineered to personify unhipness, the result would be Marilynne Robinson. . . . Ah well. I will only grow older." Robinson, *What Are We Doing Here?*, 135. In her earlier writings, she was warned off religion as not being very . . . "cool." Robinson, *The Death of Adam*, 261. Imagine if she had heeded those warnings? She would have betrayed her own soul and literature would have lost the spiritual depth of *Housekeeping* and the Gilead cycle.

65 Robinson, *When I Was a Child I Read Books*, 125.
66 Larsen and Johnson, *Balm in Gilead*, x.
67 Contemporaneous notes from the event.
68 Larson and Johnson, *Balm in Gilead*, ix.
69 Robinson, *Gilead*, 94–96; *Home*, 196; *Lila*, 251; *Jack*, 161–62.
70 Robinson, *The Givenness of Things*, 159.
71 Robinson, *The Givenness of Things*, 133.
72 Robinson, *The Death of Adam*, 261. "There are countless good souls in the mainline churches. No other tradition interests or attracts me." Robinson, *The Givenness of Things*, 101.
73 Robinson, *The Death of Adam*, 227–29.
74 Robinson, *What Are We Doing Here?*, 308.
75 Robinson, *The Givenness of Things*, 101.
76 See, for instance, her essays "Theology," in Robinson, *The Givenness of Things*, 209–25, and "Theology for This Moment," in Robinson, *What Are We Doing Here?*, 35–49. Her theological musings are scattered throughout her essays, however.
77 Robinson, *What Are We Doing Here?*, 313.
78 Robinson, *The Givenness of Things*, 275.

3

Wandering Souls in *Housekeeping*

Loneliness is an absolute discovery.

—Marilynne Robinson, *Housekeeping*

Robinson's debut novel, *Housekeeping*, landed on the literary landscape in 1980, making an immediate impact that still reverberates today. It received widespread critical recognition, winning the PEN/Hemingway award for Best First Novel, as well as being short-listed for the Pulitzer Prize, among other accolades.[1] Even more remarkably, Robinson never intended to publish it: "It was kind of a joke with me how completely unpublishable I felt I was making it."[2]

She saw it as a private exploration only her family would understand, laced with childhood memories and family lore.[3] Eventually a friend sent the manuscript to a publisher and the rest is history. Moreover, she began to write it in graduate school at the University of Washington while she was completing her dissertation on Shakespeare.[4] The demands and deadlines of graduate school clearly did not stifle her creativity, nor did her dissertation advisor dissuade her.[5] Ironically, she shudders at the prospect of rereading her dissertation, while her side-project launched her career and continues to be assigned in colleges and universities around the world.[6]

The story began with a dream. As she slept in the library, she dreamt of "a catastrophic train accident," which she wrote down.[7] She also wrote extended metaphors on looseleaf paper. When she taught in France after her graduation, she coalesced these extended metaphors with her dream.[8] The final product retained its surreal quality, as Walter Percy's endorsement expresses: "*Housekeeping* is a haunting dream of a story told in a language as sharp and clear as light and air and water."[9] Its surrealism, at both artistic and metaphysical levels, reflects Robinson's expressionistic writing style: "In my fiction my characters are not simulations of 'actual people,' whatever they are. They're much more like figures in dreams to me," each with their own "emotional logic" rather than literal or realistic representations.[10] In light of its surrealism, sweeping landscape, and intense interiority, Robinson thought the novel would be "unfilmable," just as she thought it would be "unpublishable," but in

1987 it was made into a film.[11] Robinson visited the set and approved the enterprise: "She said it was like stepping into her dreams."[12]

A book as nuanced and complex as *Housekeeping* defies pithy synopsis. At a narrative level, it traces the aftermath of a series of family tragedies. The diving of the derailed train into Fingerbone lake forms the striking symbolic center of the story. Compounding family losses—grandfather, grandmother, mother, and eventually sister—haunts the narrator, Ruth. Along with her sister Lucille and aunt Sylvie, they form an unconventional family that increasingly worries the community as they ignore and defy its basic conventions. At a character level, it is a story of Ruth's coming of age in the American West, where her consciousness of self, context, and place expands throughout. Artistically, Robinson desired to create a world of "femaleness" in the West, not as an artistic act of animus toward men, but as a celebration of women's place in the West and as a corrective to their absence or underrepresentation in literature on the West.[13]

Like any classic, *Housekeeping* can be read from many different interpretive angles: "Literary critics found rich material in analyzing how themes of transience, absence, presence, loneliness, convention, and resistance play out in the gendered spaces of home that *Housekeeping* explores."[14] Some see it as a "trauma narrative," a story about loss and its transfigurations.[15] Others emphasize its echoes of American transcendentalism thematically (return to nature, critique of society) and stylistically (the pervasiveness of metaphor and symbolism).[16] Feminist readings of *Housekeeping* focus on its repudiation of the domestic realm, famously epitomized in the burning of the family home near the end of the narrative.[17] Others view it through the lens of "religious asceticism," reading Sylvie and Ruth as renunciants, breaking free from the constraints of society.[18] We would expect a proliferation of interpretations from a text so layered and lyrical. It is not our task to adjudicate between these and other interpretations—of course they all capture aspects of the novel—or to develop a new theory, but, rather, to explore its insights into the life of the soul.

At a spiritual level, *Housekeeping* ruminates on the nature of consciousness and poses the question: What do we do with our solitude? More pointedly, it asks: How do we reconcile or fail to reconcile our solitude with the demands of society, the traumas of our past, and the souls that pull us in different directions? How do we live our solitude authentically and meaningfully amid these experiential crosscurrents? These sub-questions take us into the spiritual realm of the life of the soul. How do we hear the spiritual music of the novel? Robinson thinks of writing as music,[19] so it is not surprising she likens her novel to a song: "I always thought of *Housekeeping* as a song, never as a sociological or psychological model. I wanted to give the place a music that would evoke its atmosphere—which has more to do with vastness and emptiness than with the lives lived on its edges."[20] Let us now tune our ears to the spiritual melodies of her song.

The core characters of *Housekeeping* are wanderers, geographically and—more fundamentally—spiritually.

Edmund, the almost-absent family patriarch, wanders from his subterranean home to the mountains.[21] His three daughters—Molly, Helen, and Sylvie—wander away from Fingerbone: Molly to China via San Francisco, Helen to Seattle, and Sylvie to several locations, including Montana,[22] to the point of transience.[23] Ruth and Lucille wander by the lake and in the forest. Ruth also wanders in thought, a family characteristic. By the end of the novel, Lucille has probably left town, perhaps for Boston, as she intimated earlier,[24] while her aunt and sister seem to wander the West as freighthoppers, perhaps as ghosts.[25] They all wander, but in different directions and in diverse ways. To capture the spiritual notes of their wandering, we must attend to each character in turn, consider their attempts to come to terms with their lives, and glean conclusions about what their modes of consciousness and action in the world teach about the spiritual life.

Helen, Ruth and Lucille's mother, seems trapped inside herself, imprisoned by an unaccountable despair that leads to her suicide. She leaves no note, no explanation for why she could no longer endure existence.[26] When she flew off the cliff in her car to sail into Fingerbone lake, she took with her the secrets of herself, leaving only questions for her mother, sisters, and daughters.[27] Why would she abandon them? Why were they not enough for her to turn the car around? Her mother might have wondered how she had failed her, how she contributed to her troubled state of mind. Helen might not have been able to articulate her feelings: "It was as if she righted herself continually against some current that never ceased to pull."[28] Moreover, she might not have known the source of her anguish, or any remedies other than self-annihilation. Lost in the silence of despair, shackled by a life that seemed foreign to her, and crushed by disappointments, she plunges toward oblivion rather than stay one more day in a life she could not inhabit. Helen raises the sadly familiar struggle with the darkness of despondency, a struggle that ranges from clinical depression to spiritual desolation to emotional despair to many combinations of these and similar states of mind. Those who have experienced the darkness directly know its devastating impact on themselves and others.

Every serious writer of spirituality must confront the dark night of the soul: the experience of spiritual and emotional desolation that besets most souls at some point in their life. It is so common, in fact, that you might view it as a spiritual rite of passage, a mark of spiritual progress. For some, the dark night of the soul extends for days, for others, a lifetime. The spiritual life acknowledges this darkness and disorientation, knows its debilitations, and points to the unrelenting love of God even amidst the darkness, even to those who cannot see or feel it. On the cross, Christ experiences despair, famously uttered in his cry of dereliction: "My God, my God, why have you forsaken me?"[29] While despair feels like divine abandonment, God stays close to the brokenhearted.[30] We never know what fueled Helen's despair: Was it a genetic predisposition, relational heartache, the stresses of single motherhood, or an indistinct sense of untetheredness to this world? Maybe it was none of these, or maybe a combination, but in the end she succumbed to the hopelessness that grew in her, as many souls do, which calls for compassion and grace. Those who perish from hidden battles deserve as much honor, respect, and admiration as those who fall in open warfare. They fought bravely too, even though the battles were internal, unwitnessed.

Andrew Cunning rightly identifies a central theme of the novel: "*Housekeeping* is, above all, about loss."[31] Helen hovers in the background, haunting the minds of her bereft daughters, reappearing in the resemblances of her closest kin. Ruth remarks that Sylvie "reminded me of my mother more and more."[32] Sylvie says of Ruth: "She's her mother all over again."[33] Ruth finds herself thinking about her mother frequently. Out of the blue her mother will come to mind, a memory, or a realization: "She was a music I no longer heard, that rang in my mind, itself and nothing else, lost to all sense, but not perished, not perished."[34] As Ruth poetically expresses, loss does not entail the erasure of the person who dies. Physically, they are absent, no longer walking beside us, no longer sharing good times and bad, no longer being themselves in this world. Spiritually, however, they are present in our memories, in the lives they have touched, in their family members. In fact, death only renders Helen more present and vivid imaginatively and emotionally. In life she was often inaccessible; in death, she is always immediately accessible.

Love binds souls together for life, and death does not sever that sacred bond. Instead, it transposes it to a spiritual key, creating new music, often melancholic, but sometimes still joyful. Death forces us to sing a new song, one that incorporates the melodies of the person who died, and the tones of our grief. Death forces us to renegotiate reality, to work around their absence, but never to forget them, never to "move on" from them because they are always with us. We can *never* "move on" (a pernicious injunction as it relates to grief) because they will always remain a part of us, despite their physical absence. This deep spiritual truth does not diminish the weight of their absence, however. We still miss them so much, and miss so much about them: their laugh, voice, smell, and touch. What would we give for another embrace, talk, even just an average day together, enjoying the simple pleasures of leisurely time together? What would we give to say "hello" or "I'm sorry" or "I love you" one more time? It is beyond reckoning.

In Helen, then, we discover several salient truths about the spiritual life. Many souls struggle, often in silence. This calls for compassion, for reaching out beyond the walls of the self, to enter the pain of someone else, to try to help, as her friend Beatrice did, or just to sit with someone in their despair without judgment, without answers, with only our supportive presence. It is important to normalize the dark night of the soul, not to stigmatize it as aberrant or unspiritual. If you are in that darkness right now know that it is not forever. There are points of light for you to follow if you lift your eyes up from the abyss and look at the horizon, at the mountains, at the sky. If you know someone in that darkness offer whatever help you can, whether it is in the form of information about medical health professionals they might consult, or anecdotes about others who have shared a similar experience, or just you and your willingness to be in it with them.

We also learn from Helen about identity formation as it relates to loss. Ruth is a motherless daughter through death, a fatherless daughter through abandonment, and eventually a sisterless sister through defection. She processes these losses, sometimes through the evasion of abstraction, sometimes through the retreat into her mind, sometimes through the transference of her love and sorrow to another, such as Sylvie. These losses define her and give her an opportunity to forge a new identity, positively reinscribing them into her life through acceptance, forgiveness, and new beginnings. Helen's story may end early in the narrative, but the impact of it echoes through the pages of the novel, never disappearing because she remains dear to those she left behind. Helen teaches us that we are defined by our losses and how we respond to them. How we live with loss forms us spiritually.

Finally, Helen gives us a glimpse into a central motif of Robinson's writings: mystery. Life is a mystery. Other souls are a deep mystery, inaccessible to us in their entirety. Ruth, her own daughter, did not understand Helen: "My mother was happy that day, we did not know why. And if she was sad the next, we did not know why. And if she was gone the next, we did not know why."[35] Sylvie, her sister, had difficulty sketching her: "It's hard to describe someone you know so well."[36] Even those closest to you, those you love the most and know the most, cannot be fully captured or comprehended: there is always a surplus of being beyond your perception. Mystery requires respect for the hiddenness of others and reserve with our sense of familiarity. We do not know the private pain of others or their secret joys. Mystery means incomplete knowledge of and intimacy with others, even while it promises the endless joy of discovery.

Sylvie, Lucille and Ruth's aunt, is the younger sister of Helen and similarly elusive and inward-looking.[37] Whereas Helen attempted to live in society and raise a family, Sylvie seems to opt for the open road. She hops trains from place to place, free as a bird, happy as a leaf surfing the wind. To outsiders, she is a transient and thereby suspect. Homeless, wandering, she refuses to bow to society's conventions. Her style of life seems less a protest and more of an embrace of her free spirit, her immersion in the moment, and her disregard for the implicit and explicit mores of society. She wanders in the wilderness alone, "borrows" the boat on the shore, walks on the train tracks just for the experience, and seems keenly interested in the stories of others. Most of the time she seems oblivious to her transgressions of social conventions but, at other times, she complies with them, at least perfunctorily, if she feels that it is necessary.

We see in Sylvie a representation of a free spirit, unbounded by societal strictures, family obligations, and interpersonal expectations. Free spirits drink deeply from this life, gathering experiences and stories, witnessing beautiful landscapes and meeting fascinating people. We all know people who operate outside of the regular systems of society. They enthrall us with their exciting life, dazzle us with their tales, but also sometimes infuriate us with their unreliability or inability to fulfil what seem like basic economic and social obligations, like paying bills or arriving on time. Free spiritedness comes at a cost, both to the person and to those who love them. What they gain in adventure and variety they lose in stability and situatedness. When Sylvie comes to town, the bereaved sisters worry almost immediately that she will leave, and of course she does eventually leave, literally in a blaze of glory. The pull of the open road (or rail) lures her away from a settled life, calling her to new adventures and places. Free spirits desire an unfettered, untethered life where every day brings a new adventure in new places with new faces.

Free spirits like Sylvie generate conflict without knowing it, or knowing why it follows them like a shadow. We never learn why Sylvie Fisher does not live with her husband.[38] Her mother cut her from her will and winces at the mention of her name.[39] The man whose boat she steals screams at her from the shore.[40] Free spirits operate with a sense of innocence, living in the moment, soaking in life, but at a cost to others: those they leave behind, those they rely on for practical needs, and those who miss them. Freedom is never free; it always costs someone something, even if you never see the bill. So if the conventional world feels foreign to you, or oppressive, or boring, and if you long for new vistas then you might be a free spirit. Sail away then, for you must be the soul you are, but be mindful of those who remain anchored, and visit from time to time to share your tales of the sea, and to thank those who helped you sail.

With Lucille, the current flows in the opposite direction: toward a settled, conventional home life. From the start of her interactions with Sylvie, she resists any suggestion of the open road. When Sylvie recounts the pleasures of train travel, she suggests that she could take them with her on a railway adventure: "Take us where?," Lucille asks, foreshadowing their eventual split.[41] Lucille scolds Sylvie for deviant—particularly transient—behavior: her attire, sleeping on a bench, walking on the railway bridge.[42] Unlike her aunt and sister, Lucille is drawn to the stability of society and its constructions: "In the spring I had begun to sense that Lucille's loyalties were with the other world."[43] She longs for the company of others.[44] She begins to conform to society's expectations and insist her sister and aunt do the same. She wonders about Sylvie's husband and asks indelicately why she did not have children.[45] As Sylvie and Ruth drift away from society, with its rules and routines and regulations, Lucille slowly drifts toward it.

Lucille, then, internalizes society's mores and expectations. Rather than resist and defy them, she embraces them and pressures her family to conform, to become more "normal." When they become increasingly socially deviant and conspicuous, Lucille leaves, a repudiation and rejection of their idiosyncratic life, which she exchanges for an ostensibly ordinary life. She moves in with her single home economics teacher: "Miss Royce gave her the spare room. In effect, she adopted her, and I had no sister after that night."[46] Lucille no longer interacts with Ruth at school, given her new socially conscious sensibilities.[47] She exchanges her family home—with its eccentricities, history, and traumas—for a new home, a blank slate in which to craft her new identity. Sylvie devises a plan to lure Lucille back, at least for a visit, by employing the most basic social convention: a meal together.[48] The meal never happens. Lucille breaks free from them to start anew.

Ironically, Lucille's determination to operate within the confines of society came after an experience of its injustice. "But one morning she was accused of looking over someone's shoulder during a history test. . . . Lucille was much too indifferent to school ever to be guilty of cheating."[49] The false accusation disconcerted her: "Lucille was astonished to find that the teacher was so easily convinced of her guilt, so immovably persuaded of it, calling her up in front of the class. . . . Lucille writhed under this violation of her anonymity."[50] This led to a period of truancy, after which Lucille would decide finally to make peace with society rather than reject it. To protect herself from the world's withering gaze, she decides to join ranks with it. In a similar way, to prevent another abandonment, she lives with a surrogate mother and in all probability will eventually become a mother herself, "snuggling pretty daughters in her lap."[51]

Representationally, Lucille signifies the homesteading soul, that is, the soul that opts for stability, situatedness, and standardization. Souls of this sensibility value routine, predictability, and safety. Positively, they gain a pattern of life that insulates them from the uncertainty and risk of the open road. They build families and communities that enrich life. They come to the end of their days knowing who they were and where they belonged. Negatively, they lose the thrill of adventure, the expansiveness of discovering new people and places, and the realization of constant change that the road affords. Neither is inherently good or bad or preferable: it is not a moral question; it is an existential question. Neither is it absolute: some balance homesteading with the open road by vacationing in exotic locations and open roading with homesteading by developing "home bases" where they can regroup and refuel themselves for the road.

Spiritually, these contrasting impulses reveal two configurations of the relationship between the self and others. The one privileges the value of solitude in the expression of the self, while the other privileges community. Souls are formed by both. On the one hand, every soul must confront their solitude, must take stock of their interiority and determine the meaning of their particularity. To answer the question "Who am I?" the soul must look inward. No one else can answer that question for them. On the other hand, souls cannot answer that question in total isolation from the people and places that have formed them. To answer the question "Who am I?" the soul must look back at their personal and family history and around at their social context. The soul finds itself in solitude and community, but these poles balance differently for everyone.

"My name is Ruth."[52] *Housekeeping* begins with this disarmingly straightforward staccato introduction, echoing "Call me Ishmael," *Moby-Dick*'s starting note.[53] Names tell us nothing and everything. "Ruth" is a biblical name, but

Robinson's "Ruth" is not religious. Nevertheless, her name carries symbolic significance: "It establishes," Engebretson says, "the biblical book of Ruth as a narrative, symbolic, and characterological template."[54] Robinson herself associates it with the themes in the book of Ruth.[55] These themes include loss, grief, displacement, and compassion.[56] The biblical Ruth's loss of her husband and subsequent devotion to her mother-in-law Naomi casts light on *Housekeeping*'s Ruth's devotion to her aunt Sylvie. It is a devotion borne out of loss and displacement, a commitment of translated love. Biblical imagery and metaphors abound in *Housekeeping* and yet it is not overtly theological.[57] The spiritual and theological insights are embedded in the images, metaphors, and relationships, not in the biblical allusions.

Who is Ruth? She is the eldest of two daughters born to a troubled mother. Abandoned by her father, orphaned by her mother, and then bereaved by her grandmother, she faces the successive losses of parents and parental figures. Emotionally, she is deeply interior. Is her intense inwardness an epiphenomenon of loss and trauma, a genetic heritage, a learned behavior, or simply a personality trait? In a sense, the origin of her interiority does not matter. For whatever reason or combination of reasons, she lives within herself, at a psychological distance from external reality. If she knew her interiority was a trauma response, a retreat from inhospitable reality, she would still traverse the world from outside of it. If she discovered she inherited a depressive gene or tendency from her mother and grandfather, it would not alter the dark side of her solitude. If she realized that it was simply her inner constitution, her comportment would not change. Knowledge of origins does not fundamentally alter identity, although it can illuminate it in ways that can be beneficial.

Ruth experiences the world from the outside, watching it, venturing into it only tentatively and temporarily, as an outsider rather than as an inhabitant: "It was a source of both terror and comfort to me then that I often seemed invisible—incompletely and minimally existent, in fact. It seemed to me that I made no impact on the world, and that in exchange I was privileged to watch it unawares."[58] Sometimes she feels her existence only slightly, almost as an intrusion. She walks through town with her head tilted down, not meeting the eyes of passersby. In nature, she feels herself peering from the outside as well, the depths of the lake almost calling her to the bottom, the darkness consuming her. Lying by the lake, she felt herself absorbed in nature: "I simply let the darkness in the sky become coextensive with the darkness in my skull and bowels and bones."[59] If "[d]arkness is the only solvent," the stain must be existence itself, with its untold losses, with its indignities and injustices, with its unfair distribution of happiness.[60] The contraction of her outer life corresponds to the capaciousness of her inner life as she expands inwardly

As the world closes in, Ruth retreats into abstractions, and her narrations become more remote, more disconnected from reality. Once Sylvie revealed to the well-meaning ladies of the town that they were out all night and spent part of it in a little boat, intervention became inevitable. "I knew we were doomed."[61] That realization plunges her into a biblical meditation on loss: "Cain murdered Able, and blood cried out from the earth; the house fell on Job's children, and a voice was induced or provoked into speaking from a whirlwind; and Rachel mourned for her children; and King David for Absalom."[62] From these biblical allusions she draws a metaphysical conclusion: "The force behind the movement of time is a mourning that will not be comforted."[63] The sudden influx of biblical references and theological conclusions marks a shift in her consciousness, an almost absolute turn inward. Loss is inextricably woven into the tapestry of the world, into the fabric of her reality: "I cannot taste a cup of water but I recall that the eye of the lake is my grandfather's, and that the lake's heavy, blind, encumbering waters composed my mother's limbs and weighed her garments and stopped her breath and stopped her sight."[64]

Spiritually, Ruth illustrates the joys and revelations of solitude. Ruth's reveries are a window into her soul. In solitude we encounter ourselves unmediated by others, unencumbered by social expectations and obligations. When we are alone with ourselves we confront an unfiltered version of ourselves, the version masked by social roles and inflected by various contexts that accent selected facets of the self. Solitude strips away performativity and leaves us with just us, with all our faults, insecurities, and doubts on the one side and joys, dreams, and capacities on the other. Self-knowledge requires spending time with ourselves, listening to the thoughts and feeling the emotions that lie deeply buried. Ruth has unexpressed grief over the loss of her mother that surfaces in moments of solitude, where she begins to imagine her. Sylvie, in a similar vein, talks a lot about other people's children, perhaps an indication of her sensitivity over her childlessness, or perhaps indicating a loss of a child. Only time alone, traveling the inner recesses of the self, can reveal the hidden currents that require surfacing for self-knowledge and self-actualization.

"Loneliness is an absolute discovery," Ruth muses.[65] Robinson echoes this sentiment an interview: "Loneliness is a radical experience of self. Or soul."[66] In Christian spirituality, the desert fathers detail the psychological and emotional bombardment that assails souls in solitude. We might not like what we see or want to unearth what we have buried in the soil of our psyche. Our strategies of self-evasion are endless. Contemporary life, dominated and defined by cell phones, TVs, and all manner of technological modes of engagement, make it all too easy to avoid time alone with ourselves. In fact, our consciousness can become almost entirely mediated through technology and social media. When that happens, we displace our true self with the version we are fronting, and, perhaps worse, lose track of which self we really are. In all the posing and posturing, angling and choreographing, the true self disappears, buried in performativity. By the end of our days, we can have documented, staged, and shared our life virtually without really living it at all from the inside. Virtual curation results in self-estrangement: the loss of an authentic sense of self in the effort to perform a socially rewarded version of ourselves.

Now this sounds a little temperamental—"grumpy old man syndrome"—and it is in part. Old folks critique the innovations they find irksome, but we must not let that tendency, relived in every generation, furnish us with grounds to dismiss it entirely. Ruth's inwardness tells us about her preoccupations, but also her self-deceptions. It is not only difficult to be alone with ourselves because it forces us to come to terms with our true self. It is also difficult because total self-honesty is nearly impossible. We all tell ourselves stories about ourselves that are skewed, often in our favor. Once we are finally alone with ourselves, how do we identify and expose our self-delusions, self-illusions, and false narratives? The only way out of our inveterate capacity for self-deception is to check our stories about ourselves against others. Do our loved ones tell a different story about us? Do our enemies capture a truth we refuse to see? Do our counsellors, clergy, and therapists identify patterns of behavior that elude us? The self in total isolation will fall into psychic traps without others to help it sidestep them. Souls can only find themselves in solitude, but they can only validate and express their self-knowledge in community.

Housekeeping also invites reflection on the permeability of souls, the sense of spiritual interchangeability. Robinson reveals the symbolic unity of her three protagonists: "I don't even consider Sylvie, Ruth, and Lucille fully distinct characters. They are a suite of impulses—yearnings, regrets, loyalties, intentions—that could occur together in one mind. I thought of them in this way as I wrote it . . ."[67] Ruth describes her and Lucille as "a single consciousness."[68] By the end of the novel, however, after Lucille leaves, Sylvie and Ruth's consciousnesses merge: "Sylvie and I (I think that night we were almost a single person)."[69] Flashes of permeability are scattered throughout: Sylvie mistakes Ruth for Lucille,[70] Ruth whispers "Helen" to Sylvie,[71] and Sylvie says of Ruth, "She's her mother all over again"[72] and "Now I look at Ruthie and I see Helen too."[73] Souls collide and combine throughout *Housekeeping*, sometimes through a shared family history, sometimes through shared experiences, and sometimes through shared sensibilities. What is the significance of these transmutations and transfigurations?

Spiritually, moments of internalization and identification transport us through a heightened sense of unity and belonging. Those closest to us, who spiritually sync with us, keep the marauding sense of isolation at bay. Like any euphoric experience, however, dangers lurk nearby. If the identification grows too absolute, it compromises the individuality of both persons. As two souls merge, they diminish and eventually destroy the distinctive markers that define them, since the absorption in and with the other person comes at the cost of cultivating their uniqueness, of affirming their particularity, of realizing their individual destiny. They sacrifice their singularity in the union. Consciousnesses must individuate to activate their distinctive purpose, so while the soul's permeability allows others to pass through us and meld with us temporarily, we must guard against codependency, overexposure, and the abdication of agency.

When we are enraptured with someone who begins to define our identity, it can become totalizing and obsessive.

That, too, has potential pitfalls. If we are consumed by any single relationship, however enriching and even defining, it can lead to insularity. Lucille expresses this concern to Ruth: "We've spent too much time together. We need other friends."[74] Investing in one relationship to the exclusion of others limits us emotionally and experientially. Ruth is under the influence of Lucille for a time and then Sylvie, both of whom influence her behavior and shape her perspective. Better, then, to diversify emotional investments, to have a handful of meaningful relationships that access different facets of ourselves. If, for instance, we were overly dependent on our relationship with our mother, we might not know the joys of spousal intimacy, or of a strong friendship, or of a creative collaboration. Lucille ultimately expands her relational horizon, but Ruth and Sylvie contract their social life to one another, which ultimately has disastrous consequences for their individual flourishing and for Lucille, who must have felt abandoned again.

Just as Ruth ties herself first to Lucille and then to Sylvie as her social anchor, so also our primary relationships change throughout life. Think of the child's primary relationship with its parents, which then switches to friends, often cycling between friends, then to girlfriends and boyfriends, then to a spouse, then perhaps to a new spouse after a death or divorce. In their turn and for their time, each relationship will activate the soul in different ways, accent different aspects of it, and open and close growth possibilities. What if Ruth had allowed her principal Mr. French to guide her development as a trusted authority figure?[75] What if she had moved with her sister to Miss Royce's? Different people expand our emotional and spiritual possibilities, even as a primary relationship anchors us emotionally and spiritually. Let us recognize, then, the force of these bonds, the cost, and the probability that we will cycle through several throughout our life as we grow and change.

All changes disrupt. They disrupt our schedules, routines, relationships, and sense of self in proportion to their significance. When we alternate between "soulmates," expect turbulence. The person we move away from will often react with hostility, sadness, and confusion. Ruth and Sylvie illustrate this well when they begin to distance themselves from each other. Conflict naturally ensues. They fight about the flowers in their grandfather's dictionary. Ruth, always drawn to nature and books, finds them intriguing, Lucille shakes them out, foreshadowing her rejection of the family's eccentricities.[76] Similarly Lucille becomes absorbed in making a dress, a sign of her embrace of convention, while Ruth refuses to help.[77] They reconcile after the episode, but it is a harbinger of things to come. Ruth finds herself unable or unwilling to follow Lucille on her path toward social acceptability, and Lucille reacts with hostility and distancing.[78] We can expect similar tensions and conflict during times of relational transition, which calls for patience with the process, both with the person undergoing the change and with those impacted by it.

Other than a steaming train diving into an icy lake, which, as Ruth says, "was not, strictly speaking, spectacular, because no one saw it happen,"[79] the most spectacular moment in *Housekeeping* is when Ruth and Sylvie set the family home ablaze: "Sylvie set fire to the straw of the broom, and held it blazing to the hem of the pantry curtain, and to the fringe of the rug, so there were two good fires . . ."[80] Many see this act as a repudiation of the domestic realm: "The burning of the house, which is often read as a radical feminist gesture, is perhaps best seen as Ruth and Sylvie's last act of purgation."[81] They lit the fire with domestic instruments against domestic objects. Their act liberates them from the daily grind of domesticity, which had become untenable: "Now truly we were cast out to wander, and there was an end to housekeeping."[82] Neither felt called to or well suited for the domestic life, so rather than perform it for the approval of others, they leave it all behind.

Spiritually, the scene—and they surely "made a scene"—speaks to the imperative to pursue authenticity. If they had stayed and made a life in Fingerbone that was completely at odds with their authentic selves, the result would have been interminable misery and self-betrayal. Perhaps that was how Ruth's grandmother felt, how many grandmothers have felt through the centuries: trapped, dissatisfied, unactualized, bitter. To stay would have betrayed their shared sense of displacement and their bond, since Ruth was soon to be taken away. Their life in the family home in Fingerbone had devolved into mere theater, pacification, and mollification. Sylvie performed the duties of domesticity with gusto: "Those days she cast about constantly for ways to conform our lives to the expectations of others, or to what she guessed their expectations might be, and she was full of purpose, which sometimes seemed like hope."[83] In a final frenzy of domesticity, a final attempt to fit into society, to allay concerned community members, "neighbor women and church women,"[84] and placate authorities—the sheriff and the judge—she threw herself into the caregiver role expected of her, but to no avail. She could not change the drift of her life in a frantic, forced effort at social conformity. It was too foreign to her wandering disposition. It was bound to fail, and it did.

In the end, they chose to abscond from society rather than live an inauthentic life. Authenticity, however, comes at a price. You must purge parts of yourself, sometimes valued parts, and even your past to become something new. If society has boxed you into a role, to break free will cause damage. Purgation, as a preparatory step to higher spiritual stages, is a mainstay in Christian spirituality. Typically applied to sin, it can also apply to the dross that accumulates in an inauthentic life. We acquire habits, things, and even relationships that we must leave behind before we can soar spiritually. We must burn our inauthentic self to the ground before we can construct something new, something authentic and lasting, and that will cost us and others—sometimes dearly. We must leave a life behind, parts of which we still cherish, before we can create a new life, and that is exactly what Ruth and Sylvie did. Imagine how Lucille must have felt at the news of their final acts? Betrayed? Abandoned? Retraumatized? Spiritual growth will cost us and others in unforeseen ways, but out of the ashes of an inauthentic life something beautiful can arise.

Finally, presence and absence, particularly presence through absence, runs throughout *Housekeeping* as a dominant chord. "Readers of *Housekeeping* quickly learn to find the presence of Helen's absence on every page."[85] Helen is absently present in life and presently absent in death.[86] Her suicide permeates the consciousness of all the characters, especially her daughters. In Ruth's ruminations she remembers and imagines Helen continually: "Say that my mother was as tall as a man, and that she sometimes set me on her shoulders, so that I could splash my hands in the leaves above my head."[87] Not all the memories are reliable, of course, and the daughters dispute their disparate versions of their mother.[88] Fingerbone lake teems with the souls of the departed, chief among them Ruth's mother and grandfather, who she imagines haunting its depths.[89] At the end of the book, the ghost consciousness of Ruth imagines Lucille shaped by their loss, her thoughts "thronged by our absence."[90] They haunt and are haunted.

Two key spiritual principles arise from the theme of absence. First, as it relates to bereavement, the souls of the dearly departed never fully leave us because they are grafted into our hearts. Ironically, their physical absence often heightens their spiritual presence, either at a metaphorical or metaphysical level. We feel them more keenly sometimes afterwards as we take stock of their life and their significance to us. As their life shaped the landscape of our hearts, so their loss reshapes it. Their departure transforms our daily experience, forcing us to renegotiate reality and reconfigure our identity. They still reside in our imagination and recollections and they still define our identity, at least in part. We are always the product of the loss, the person formed by it, named anew. Ruth was always a daughter who lost a mother and her mother never sunk away completely into the lake. Souls we love do not fade away completely when they pass away. Instead, we still see their faces in our mind's eye and we continue to relate to them in new, more interior ways.

Second, the theme of the relationship between presence and absence invites reflection on the ways in which we are present and absent in life. In *Housekeeping* many of the characters are aloof, emotionally and practically disconnected from others. Helen does not talk much in the car ride to Fingerbone.[91] Sylvie stands alone in the dark flood waters, unresponsive to Ruth.[92] Ruth does not talk to Lucille on the way to school.[93] It seems that quiet abstraction and rumination runs in Ruth's family, distancing them from those around them. They often live more in their heads than in the world around them. Now, nothing is wrong with quiet, removed, intentional introspection—this study is an exercise in it—but presence requires coming out of the recesses of the self to encounter the world of others, even when it feels uncomfortable or intimidating. For reflective souls, it often takes more effort than for souls more naturally in the moment. For all, the practice of presence entails attending to the people and the places around you. Love is benevolent attention. Love is giving what you are and what you have in this very moment to the people around you: nothing more, nothing less. That is presence.

Conclusion

Housekeeping explores the nature of consciousness and the complex processes by which the soul in its solitude navigates the outside world. It illustrates the continual negotiation of the self with others and its environment and experience, especially traumatic experiences. Souls must decide to what extent they will internalize and thus accommodate society, with its expectations and obligations, and to what extent they will resist its conventions and coercions. Every soul must traverse the space between its solitude and society, must come to terms with its tragedies and trauma, and must find a way to make a home in the world. *Housekeeping* does not offer a normative vision: it does not recommend one way of life over another. For instance, it does not promote an itinerant life over a settled life. Instead, it shows the explicit and implicit interconnections between souls, and the implications of their life choices for themselves and others. The novel invites reflection on the ways we conform to and deviate from societal norms and structures, how other souls shape us, and how to access and surface our hidden depths.

Housekeeping, as the daily effort to create hospitable and nurturing spaces, mirrors soul-keeping, that is, spiritual practices of soul care. Soul-formation requires the kind of care, attention, judiciousness, and innovation found in well-kept houses. Think of the soul as your spiritual house that needs to be swept, cleaned, cleared of clutter, and repaired. It is your "interior castle," your "inner cathedral." Regardless of nomenclature, the soul is the place where you live, a place you build or let fall into ruin, a place you adorn with beauty or deface, a place you entertain guests or reside alone. *Housekeeping* attunes us to the cold realities and stark challenges of caring for others under adverse conditions, where external pressures and internal constraints impede proper care. Similarly, those aspiring to soul-keep themselves and facilitate the spiritual flourishing of others will face adversity, including from their own limitations and blind spots.

Finally, we all have our daunting bridges to cross. Fingerbone's railroad bridge brackets the story as symbolic bookends. *Housekeeping* begins with the train derailing off the bridge "like a weasel sliding off a rock" and ends with Sylvie and Ruth's flight from town across the bridge.[94] The bridge signifies transformation. For Edmund, it ushered in the transformation from life to death, for his wife, transformation from marriage to widowhood, for his children, fatherlessness, and for the town, notoriety for the "spectacular" event. For Sylvie and Ruth, crossing the bridge signifies the rejection of society's demands and impending interventions, and the choice to stay together. Perhaps for both it was an act of loyalty to Helen since they saw Helen in each other. Bridges signify transformation, and transformation always comes with dangers, and sometimes death, at least symbolically. Old ways, patterns, and habits must die for new ones to begin. We cannot avoid bridges in life, and we cannot always know where they go, but we can tread carefully, expectantly, hopefully, and joyfully, welcoming the new terrain as it meets us on the horizon.

Notes

1 Alex Engebretson, *Understanding Marilynne Robinson* (Columbia: The University of South Carolina Press, 2017), 14.
2 Marilynne Robinson in Thomas Schaub, "An Interview with Marilynne Robinson," *Contemporary Literature* 35, no. 2 (1994): 232.
3 Robinson in Schaub, "An Interview with Marilynne Robinson," 233–34.
4 Engebretson, *Understanding Marilynne Robinson*, 14.
5 Engebretson, *Understanding Marilynne Robinson*, 14. Given the pressures on a dissertation advisor to keep one's student on track with the project, his support of her extracurricular project was impressive and, indeed, prescient.
6 "I wrote my doctoral thesis on Shakespeare, and I am very glad I did, even though, in retrospect, I think I was wrong about a great many things." She then proceeds to make the type of dry, self-effacing joke that charms her readers: "I suppose there is enough money in the world to induce me to read it again sometime, foreign currencies being taken into account." Robinson, *The Givenness of Things*, 38.
7 Engebretson, *Understanding Marilynne Robinson*, 14.
8 Engebretson, *Understanding Marilynne Robinson*, 14.
9 Listed as the first quotation of "praise for Marilynne Robinson's *Housekeeping*" in the novel.
10 Robinson in Schaub, "An Interview with Marilynne Robinson," 242.
11 *Housekeeping*, dir. Bill Forsyth (Culver City, CA: Columbia Pictures, 1987), 117 min. Robinson remarks about its unfilmability in the Indicator Blu-ray disc special feature, "Marilynne Robinson Interview," in *Housekeeping* (Culver City, CA: Columbia Pictures, 2017), 7:27. Nevertheless, she thought the movie came as close as it could to filming a book so steeped in metaphor.
12 John Pym, "Production Report," *Housekeeping*, dir. Bill Forsyth (Culver City, CA: Columbia Pictures, 1987), DVD insert, 15.
13 Robinson in Schaub, "An Interview with Marilynne Robinson," 233. In an audio interview for the fortieth anniversary of the novel, Robinson jokes that her brother calls *Housekeeping* "Moby Jane," an allusion to its dearth of male characters, inversely proportional to her favorite book, *Moby-Dick*. She also comments that she tried

to introduce a male character in the writing process, but found it "didn't work," so she removed him. Marilynne Robinson, *Housekeeping*, 40th anniv. ed., interview with Jonathan Galassi (New York: Macmillan Audiobook, 2020), disc 6, track 6. It is a celebration of the female hero rather than a protest.

14 Shannon L. Mariotti and Joseph H. Lane Jr., "Introduction: The Mystery of Experience: Marilynne Robinson's Political Theory," in *A Political Companion to Marilynne Robinson* (Lexington: The University Press of Kentucky, 2016), 7.

15 Laura E. Tanner, *The Elusive Everyday in the Fiction of Marilynne Robinson* (New York: Oxford University Press, 2021), 30; Andrew Cunning, *Marilynne Robinson, Theologian of the Ordinary* (New York: Bloomsbury Academic, 2021), 36.

16 Cunning, *Marilynne Robinson, Theologian of the Ordinary*, 26–27; Engebretson, *Understanding Marilynne Robinson*, 14: "*Housekeeping* appropriates and refashions tropes and stylistic tendencies from American Romanticism, primarily the work of Melville, Dickinson, Thoreau, and Emerson."

17 Engebretson, *Understanding Marilynne Robinson*, 15–16, 25.

18 Engebretson, *Understanding Marilynne Robinson*, 15.

19 Robinson, *When I Was a Child I Read Books*, 130.

20 Marilynne Robinson, "An Interview with Marilynne Robinson," in *This Life, This World: New Essays on Marilynne Robinson's "Housekeeping," "Gilead," and Home,"* ed. Jason W. Stevens (Leiden: Brill, 2016), 258.

21 Marilynne Robinson, *Housekeeping* (New York: Farrar, Straus & Giroux, 1980), 4.

22 Robinson, *Housekeeping*, 39, 216.

23 Robinson, *Housekeeping*, 10, 14.

24 Robinson, *Housekeeping*, 132.

25 Robinson, *Housekeeping*, 216–17.

26 Robinson, *Housekeeping*, 20.

27 Robinson, *Housekeeping*, 22.

28 Robinson, *Housekeeping*, 213.

29 Matthew 27:46.

30 Psalm 34:18.

31 Cunning, *Marilynne Robinson, Theologian of the Ordinary*, 36.

32 Robinson, *Housekeeping*, 53.

33 Robinson, *Housekeeping*, 182.

34 Robinson, *Housekeeping*, 160; cf. Robinson, *Housekeeping*, 124: "It seemed to me that what perished need not also be lost." Robinson reiterates this point in a recent interview: "One of the subjects of the book from my point of view—insofar as I am a critic—is that people do not perish in a sense, that they abide, that the mark that they put on things or the melody they create behind received reality persists, and this is very important for Ruth because she does not want to say to herself, 'this is gone, she is gone.'" Robinson, audiobook interview with Galassi, *Housekeeping*, 40th anniv. ed., disc 6, track 6.

35 Robinson, *Housekeeping*, 213; cf. 131.

36 Robinson, *Housekeeping*, 51.

37 Robinson, *Housekeeping*, 10.

38 Robinson, *Housekeeping*, 15.

39 Robinson, *Housekeeping*, 41.

40 Robinson, *Housekeeping*, 146–47.

41 Robinson, *Housekeeping*, 50.

42 Robinson, *Housekeeping*, 57, 81–82, 105. "Lucille hated everything that had to do with transience." Robinson, *Housekeeping*, 103.

43 Robinson, *Housekeeping*, 95.

44 Robinson, *Housekeeping*, 66.

45 Robinson, *Housekeeping*, 69.

46 Robinson, *Housekeeping*, 140.

47 Robinson, *Housekeeping*, 136.

48 Robinson, *Housekeeping*, 188.

49 Robinson, *Housekeeping*, 77–78.

50 Robinson, *Housekeeping*, 78.

51 Robinson, *Housekeeping*, 218.

52 Robinson, *Housekeeping*, 3.

53 Engebretson, *Understanding Marilynne Robinson*, 26.

54 Engebretson, *Understanding Marilynne Robinson*, 17.

55 Engebretson, *Understanding Marilynne Robinson*, 17.

56 Corina Crisu, "At Home with Transience: Reconfiguring Female Characters of the American West in Marilynne Robinson's *Housekeeping*," in Stevens, ed., *This Life, This World*, 43.

57 While I disagree with Cunning's characterization of Robinson as a theologian in a technical sense, her writings certainly engage theology, and demonstrate familiarity with theology. Cunning argues that her first novel sets the stage for her later theological

contributions: "Robinson's importance as a positive and constructive theologian is very much in preparation in this initial novel." Cunning, *Marilynne Robinson, Theologian of the Ordinary*, 53.

58 Robinson, *Housekeeping*, 105–6.

59 Robinson, *Housekeeping*, 116.

60 Robinson, *Housekeeping*, 116.

61 Robinson, *Housekeeping*, 190.

62 Robinson, *Housekeeping*, 192.

63 Robinson, *Housekeeping*, 192

64 Robinson, *Housekeeping*, 193–94.

65 Robinson, *Housekeeping*, 157.

66 Robinson, "An Interview with Marilynne Robinson," in Stevens, ed., *This Life, This World*, 255.

67 Robinson, "An Interview with Marilynne Robinson," in Stevens, ed., *This Life, This World*, 258.

68 Robinson, *Housekeeping*, 98.

69 Robinson, *Housekeeping*, 209.

70 Robinson, *Housekeeping*, 70.

71 Robinson, *Housekeeping*, 167.

72 Robinson, *Housekeeping*, 182.

73 Robinson, *Housekeeping*, 186.

74 Robinson, *Housekeeping*, 130.

75 Robinson, *Housekeeping*, 134–35.

76 Robinson, *Housekeeping*, 126.

77 Robinson, *Housekeeping*, 127.

78 Robinson, *Housekeeping*, 122–23.

79 Robinson, *Housekeeping*, 5–6.

80 Robinson, *Housekeeping*, 209.

81 Engebretson, *Understanding Marilynne Robinson*, 25.

82 Robinson, *Housekeeping*, 209.

83 Robinson, *Housekeeping*, 201.

84 Robinson, *Housekeeping*, 179.

85 Engebretson, *Understanding Marilynne Robinson*, 16.

86 Robinson, *Housekeeping*, 110.

87 Robinson, *Housekeeping*, 116.

88 Robinson, *Housekeeping*, 109–10.

89 Robinson, *Housekeeping*, 193–94.

90 Whether or not Sylvie and Ruth died the night of their flight from Fingerbone is an open question in the novel and remains open to

interpretation. Engebretson, *Understanding Marilynne Robinson*, 25. Despite the ambiguity, I think they died, either jumping off the bridge or falling off from a wind gust. Perhaps they do not know that they are dead, or perhaps they claim their continued reality through Lucille's memory. If they lived, they still died socially and practically, so, in a way, as it relates to Lucille at least, it amounts to the same thing: "Since we are dead, the house would be hers now." Robinson, *Housekeeping*, 217–18. Whether or not their death is legal or actual is immaterial to their absence.

91 Robinson, *Housekeeping*, 196–97.

92 Robinson, *Housekeeping*, 72.

93 Robinson, *Housekeeping*, 122.

94 Robinson, *Housekeeping*, 6, 211–16.

4

Beautiful Souls in *Gilead*

There are a thousand thousand reasons to
live this life, every one of them sufficient.

—Marilynne Robinson, *Gilead*

It all started with sublime light: "Emily Dickenson light."[1] It was Christmas in Provincetown, Massachusetts, where Robinson planned to spend the holidays with her family. In a fortuitous turn of events, her family was delayed, so she found herself alone in a hotel room under the spell of magical "sea-light," when an image came into focus that would alter the literary landscape:

> I spent days alone in an empty hotel on the tip of the continent with this amazing sea-light pouring in the window and so on . . . it's so hard to describe . . . this image came to my mind of this elderly man who I knew immediately was a pastor writing a letter to a boy that's playing on the floor by his feet . . . that's where it started, that's the initial information I had, and the whole rest of it is simply an unweaving of what was implied in that moment.[2]

From that pregnant picture *Gilead* (2004) was born, a novel which details the final days of John Ames, a Congregationalist minister in the small town of Gilead, Iowa, in the 1950s. Critics and scholars acclaimed its understated beauty. It won the Pulitzer Prize for Fiction and the National Book Critic Circle Award for Fiction.[3] Former President Barack Obama listed it as one of his favorite books, catapulting it into the public consciousness.[4] What began as a quiet vignette that dawned on her in a lonely room gradually evolved into an exquisite celebration of life and love.

In this chapter, we explore the spiritual insights embedded in *Gilead*, which, I argue, illuminates spiritually open and alert readers, transporting them to unexpected heights. How has a tale about a dying minister in a sleepy town moved so many readers? On the surface, the novel seems unpromising: it can come across as dull, remote, religious, irrelevant, and uneventful. Some readers cannot get past the first few wandering pages, which conceal the beauty that awaits. But for those who immerse themselves in the story, the tug of the deep spiritual undercurrents draws them in and carries them along for the rest of the book. The routine suddenly becomes riveting. The mundane, miraculous. As with *Housekeeping*, Robinson moves readers not through plot, but through soul. Her deep, delicate, deliberate characterization draws us in, and her deft deployment of language reaches us at subconscious levels. Without knowing exactly how, we become spiritually transfixed.

The reason is simple, although not necessarily obvious at first blush: Robinson spiritually sensitizes readers to the beauty of grace through her dying protagonist, Reverend John Ames. She shrouds this spiritual simplicity in the complexity of a life in review, where he takes stock of his ministry, relationships, and significance. In the process of explaining himself to his young son, he finds himself explaining himself *to himself*. That task turns out to be much more difficult than he might have anticipated at the outset. What has he done with his life? What was the point of the endless erudite sermons he toiled over deep into the night? Was he a tedious bore or did all the study and sermonizing benefit others? Did he acquit himself admirably in ministry or merely retreat from reality? Did he say the right things at the right moment? What legacy does he leave behind? How will his family fare once he dies? These reflective questions assume a heightened urgency as he sees the end in sight.

Like *Housekeeping*, *Gilead* resists synopsis because it accents character over plot. Events happen—tales of stolen cars, old battles, and conspicuous war wounds—but they are the background texture of Ames's self-portrait. At a basic narrative level, *Gilead* is the letter of a dying minister in a small town in Iowa to his soon-to-be bereaved son. It begins and ends abruptly: "I told you last night that I might be gone sometime, and you said, Where, and I said, To be with the Good Lord, and you said, Why, and I said, Because I'm old, and you said, I don't think you're old."[5] Then, after laying bare his life memories, with all the complex feelings they unearth, and sharing the unexpected joys and problems of his final days, as well as his hopes for his son, it ends with a promise of prayer: "I'll pray that you grow up a brave man in a brave country. I will pray you find a way to be useful. I'll pray and then I'll sleep."[6] The music between these soft notes elevates because it synchronizes the soul to the symphony of grace.

Gilead celebrates natural beauty, from vast skyscapes over endless prairies to the sight and sounds of trees at night amid moon shadows.[7] Recalling a boyhood memory of a long journey with his father to find the grave of his grandfather, Ames remembers a striking event. After many misadventures, they finally locate it. When they finish some basic landscaping—"putting things to rights"—his father bows to pray silently at length. Young Ames, tired but restless, opens his eyes and sees the skies aglow from the intermingling light of the rising moon and setting sun: "Each of them was standing on its edge, with the most wonderful light between them." Then, wanting his father to witness the beautiful light, Ames kisses his hand and says: "'Look at the moon.' And he did. We just stood there until the sun was down and the moon was up."[8] Sharing in the beauty of the fading light brought healing and hope to that difficult moment.

Beauty in *Gilead* extends beyond the natural. It also manifests in its central relationships. Ames has been cocooned in caring relationships his whole life. He basks in the glow of the love of his wife Lila and son Robby. He appreciates his best friend Robert Boughton, who accompanied him through the ups and downs of life, including the loss of Louisa and Rebecca, his first wife and child.[9] These relationships infuse his life with beauty and grace, as he tells his son: "I'm writing this in part to tell you that if you ever wonder what you've done in your life, and everyone does wonder sooner or later, you have been God's grace to me, a miracle, something more than a miracle."[10] His attentiveness to and appreciation of the beauty of relationships turns outward as well, to the beauty of young couples frolicking, young people joking, and Boughton's robust family life: "[I]t all seemed to me to be blindingly beautiful. And it was."[11] Ames spent a lifetime surrounded by relational beauty.

But beauty does not insulate Ames from suffering. In a sense, his life has been a series of losses—the loss of his wife and child early in life, the loss of his relationship with his father, the loss of opportunities for new love, a new life outside of Gilead, and, finally, the loss of his health, spiritual composure, and eventually the loss of his current wife and son through his own death. Ames has every reason to be bitter and angry at life, at himself, and at God. The pages of *Gilead*, however, are not marked by bitterness, although it does burst in from time to time when Ames reflects on his age, his impending death, or Jack's disruptive presence.[12] Instead of being consumed by anger, regret, bitterness, and the host of negative emotions he wrestles with, he strives for joy, gratitude, and celebration. Inevitably, he does not always practice what he preaches or embody these spiritual states of mind consistently, but he tries valiantly

Ames learned an important lesson about suffering and beauty early in life. He recalls a vivid memory of his father clearing away the rubble of a scorched Baptist church, victim of a lightning strike to the steeple.[13] What strikes Ames in retrospect was not the sadness of the loss of the church, its Bibles and hymnals, and the displacement of its congregation, but rather the community coming together afterwards. He saw beauty amid the ruins, beauty in the comradery, beauty in the hymn singing in the rain as they worked, beauty in the temporary suspension of social conventions—women with their hair in disrepair.[14] "It was so joyful and sad. I mention it again because it seems to me much of my life was comprehended in that moment."[15] It becomes, for Ames, a spiritually clarifying moment. It teaches him to look for beauty in suffering, and to create beauty from the ashes of life. In other words, it became spiritually paradigmatic for how to inhabit suffering in a hopeful, joyful way.

During the cleanup Ames shares a relationally significant and spiritually symbolic moment with his father. As the rain fell the ashes from the fire liquified and stuck to everything: faces, hands, and food. Ames's father brought him a biscuit that was sullied with soot: "'Never mind,' he said, 'there's nothing cleaner than ash.' But it affected the taste of biscuit, which I thought might resemble the bread of affliction . . ."[16] Ames ponders that moment and the more he ponders it, the more he realizes its spiritual salience: "That biscuit ashy from my father's charred hand. It all means more than I can tell you."[17] It takes on a sacramental quality—a visible sign of invisible grace—as if his father administered holy communion to him: "I remember it as if he broke the bread and put a bit of it in my mouth, although I know he didn't."[18] Mortality heightens the memory and meaning of the moment for him, and he searches in vain for the words to express what it means to him.

Part of the difficulty, beyond the power of words to express deep insight and the unreliability of memories laden with emotion, is the paradoxical nature of experience. Suffering is often ameliorated by small mercies. Pain is often palliated by providential provisions. To talk of a time of suffering or pain does not capture the spiritual complexity of these experiences. Ash covers it all, as suffering covers everything in hard times, but Ames finds nourishment in the biscuit, beauty in the event, and cherishes the special moment with his father, from whom he later became estranged. So when Ames finds himself plunged into the memories of "hard times," he realizes "there's a sweetness in the experience which I don't understand."[19] It is the sweetness of grace amid ruin, music in the rain, and beauty from ashes.[20] These aesthetic compensations and transformations skirt the edge of comprehension and language. How can suffering be remembered fondly?

In retrospect, is Ames happy that the Baptist church burned down? Of course not. He recognizes the loss and sadness of the event. Does Ames wish he were back in hard times? Of course not. He remembers the grief, the isolation, and the loneliness. But he comes to appreciate the inbreaking of grace in those moments. The fire and rain gave him the gift of a sacramental moment with his father and a deep spiritual insight—then only faintly understood—that would be a guiding light for him when his time of darkness came: "As you read this, I hope you will understand that when I speak of the long night that preceded these days of my happiness, I do not remember grief and loneliness so much as I do peace and comfort."[21] When lightning strikes, and fires burn, and rain falls, look for the beauty *amid* the ruin, beauty *within* the suffering, often unexpected and laced with sadness. Look for the points of light. We cannot know the joy of singing in the rain if it never rains.

Beauty lies at the heart of the spiritual life. As the soul absorbs the beauty of creation, it perceives the beauty of the Creator through it. Similarly, as the soul envelops itself in the beauty of relationships, it encounters the beauty of the *imago Dei*—the image of God—instantiated uniquely in each person. Augustine repeatedly refers to God with the terms *beautiful* and *Beauty*, underscoring the divine source of natural and relational beauty, thereby shifting the term away from the superficial to the spiritual.[22] When we see beauty, true beauty, we see a manifestation of God. God imbues the world with kaleidoscopic instances of beauty all around us, all the time. We have only to train our spiritual eyes. Like Ames, we must learn to see the beautiful in the familiar, mundane, and diurnal. From Lila's blue dress and his son's red shirt to a simple pancake breakfast, Ames discovers beauty everywhere, giving us a model to follow.[23]

Once we train our terrestrial eyes to perceive beauty, life becomes a celebration. Despite its sobering context, *Gilead* is a celebration of life. Ames continually declares how much he loves the world, loves his town, and loves his life, especially his wife and son. Early on he exclaims: "Ah, this life, this world."[24] At the very end he proclaims exuberantly: "I love this town."[25] In between he intersperses little odes to joy as he wanders through the world, enjoying small moments with friends and family, reflecting on the beauty of life, and marveling at the beauty around him. "Oh, I will miss this world."[26] The parts of the world he anticipates missing are almost always the small, seemingly unremarkable moments. Evening walks, reading in his study at night, baseball on the radio, and fried-egg sandwiches float through his mind.[27] Ames teaches us the spiritual value of celebration, appreciation, and attentiveness.

In fact, attentiveness underwrites the interconnected themes of beauty and celebration. We cannot appreciate the beauty of the natural world if we do not look up from the mundane tasks that occupy us throughout the day. Natural beauty awaits to be seen, to be explored, to be discovered. Likewise, we will never experience the beauty of relationships if we limit the scope of our attention to ourselves. Self-absorption robs us of the life-giving beauty of meaningful relationships. If we fixate on our own affairs to the exclusion of others, we imprison ourselves in a cell of self-interest. We will be spared the troubles of others, but at a grave cost. So let us reach out, enter the world of others, immerse ourselves in their experiences, and we will begin to see the beauty of others and to enjoy the beauty of relationships. Ames enjoins attentiveness to this world in all its mystery and majesty: "This is an interesting planet. It deserves all the attention you can give it."[28]

We find a touching example of the celebration of beauty in Ames's recollections of his brother Edward, his senior by ten years.[29] In contrast to Ames, Edward studied abroad, in Göttingen, and then abandoned the town and faith of his childhood.[30] Despite the tensions his atheism caused with his father, they eventually reconcile, his parents even living with him in Florida in their retirement.[31] Ames relays a fond childhood memory of playing catch with his brother, a *Field of Dreams* moment. Although Edward had become a professor of German literature and philosophy, and dressed the part, he still retained the family's love of baseball.[32] "At first he was careful of his clothes. He hadn't even seen a baseball in years, he said. But when he warmed up a little, he was pretty sharp."[33] It might seem trivial, but for Ames the spirited game of catch with his older brother demonstrated Edward's spiritual vitality, his retention of soul: "All the same, after that day I did feel pretty much at ease about the state of his soul."[34]

Edward's glove, and the special memory it represented, would stay on his desk, where it would be a daily reminder of that day and their relationship.[35] His atheism did not, in Ames's view, diminish his beauty: "He was a good man."[36] Edward serves as a good reminder that those who have departed from faith have not thereby lost their beauty, their soul. For those affiliated with institutional religion, like his father at the time, disaffiliation often signifies the imperilment or loss of soul. It is easy to write people off when you believe they have forfeited their soul, but Ames teaches us to perceive the beauty of every soul, regardless of whether their doctrinal stances align with ours. Their ultimate spiritual destiny depends on the grace of God, not our assessment, so we are free to enjoy, affirm, and appreciate them, as Ames does with Edward. Many atheists, agnostics, and "nones" have a deep sense of the spiritual life and morality.

Mortality imbues *Gilead* with gravitas, tempering the tone of celebration. Ames's terminal heart condition prompts the letter, which he writes to share family stories and impart fatherly wisdom.[37] Death's inexorable approach looms in the background not as a sword of Damocles but as an intensifier that sharpens his focus and deepens his insight. Small details that might elude the healthy and youthful take on huge significance for him: bubbles, pancakes, water, candlelight. Between his unstructured reflective reveries and recounting of memories he inserts admonitions, such as controlling his temper, especially given the family's history of anger: "I tell you so that you can watch for this in yourself."[38] Sometimes his exhortations go deeper, such as finding joy in sorrows, a lesson he learned throughout his life: "There are pleasures to be found where you would never look for them. That's a bit of fatherly wisdom."[39] As the proverbial curtains slowly close in the narrative, Ames gives his parting words of wisdom and savors every last moment of beauty given to him.

Spiritually, introspection about death, the recognition of our finitude and the desire to maximize our short time on earth, punctures the prevailing death-denialism of society. Instead of evading our existential condition, it invites a life of realism, intentionality, and appreciation. *Memento mori*—remember that you must die—is not a morbid psychology or defeatist mindset, but the basis for a philosophy of life where we learn to "number our days aright."[40] Ames's failing heart forces him to ask himself: What should I say to my son through a letter that I would want to say to him in person in the future? It forces him to embrace the life before him, the simple pleasures, the everyday joys, and to settle any outstanding relational debts. It prods him to reconcile when he fails his friends and family, and to teach, exhort, and inform his son. Ideally, the sobering knowledge of his impending death would keep him focused on the task at hand throughout his final letter.

But Ames gets off track. Rather than offer his "begats," that is, give an orderly and meaningful account of his life for the future benefit of his son, he gets pulled back into the troubles of the world, particularly the hostilities of unreconciled relationships.[41] When Jack, the prodigal son of his best friend Robert Boughton, returns to town, a chill enters the epistle. His rhapsodies on life recede into the background as does the family history he shares earlier. At first Jack's return seems like just another random detail, but soon it takes on an obsessional life of its own.

Ames himself recognizes his narrative detour: "Sometimes I almost forget my purpose in writing this."[42] He tries to course-correct, but to no avail. Jack becomes the intrusion that redirects his consciousness in his final weeks. Soon the letter uncharitably fixates on Jack, his troubled history, his uncertain motives, and Ames's failed attempts to befriend him, devolving into suspicion and acrimony before resolving into a reconciled relationship.

We can only image how his son might have read the letter twenty years later, bemused by his father's loss of focus on the initial aim of the letter: to give him a sense of his family history, to explain his unconventional situation, and to exhort and bless. Perhaps, with the benefit of hindsight, he would see it as an attempt by his father to reconcile himself to his past, including his failures with Jack. Or perhaps he would see it as his father's final attempt to convey grace through ministry, to function as a minister one last time in his counseling and blessing of Jack. Or maybe he would dismiss it as the result of advanced age, where bodily pains and discomfort combined with heightened emotion over the past and anxiety for the future prevent the kind of lucidity and coherence he might have been able to achieve in his younger years. If Robby Ames becomes anything like his father Reverend John Ames, he would see the loss of focus through the lens of grace.

Ames's diversion aptly symbolizes the nonlinear nature of the spiritual life, a life that does not move from point to point in a vertical ascent, but rather darts up and down at irregular intervals, takes unexpected detours, and culminates in different destination points. Consequently, you cannot chart the spiritual life—and spiritual growth in particular—in efficient spiritual slopes. How-to books that promise simple steps to spiritual growth might serve as a beneficial starting point, but they quickly shatter against the jagged rocks of spiritual progress and regress. Two steps forward can as easily be followed by three steps back as it can be by another step forward. There is no formula, scheme, program, or technique that can chart the trajectory of the spiritual life. To switch metaphors, the soul spirals up and down in patterns that are more often circular than straight, as Ames's repetitions, meanderings, and distractions helpfully illustrate.

Also, the distraction of Jack's return and its disruption to his designs for the letter point to another deep reality about the spiritual life. While it is natural to develop a sense of vocational direction, the people, places, and activities that occupy us often differ from our original intentions. Ames wants to focus on his son but instead broods about his godson. He wants to bless Robby but instead blesses Jack. It was not his plan. The same applies to places. Ames accepts Gilead as his spiritual vineyard, even though he might have wished for a fresh start elsewhere, out of his father's shadow, especially after the loss of his first wife and child. Life rarely allows us to choose the people, places, and activities that demand our attention and define us. You might have hoped to cultivate a particular relationship only to realize God is calling you to invest in another instead. Similarly, you might have wanted to sink roots in one location only to discover God calling you to a new place. Openness to providential disruption means that we accept that God's plans might subvert ours, as it did for Ames, and to embrace the life given rather than resent the life denied.

Acceptance means submission to God's will and trust in divine wisdom to know how to accomplish His will in and through our life. Acceptance implies neither agreement nor enthusiasm. We will need to grieve the people and places we leave behind as we pursue God's purpose for our life. We might experience a range of emotions about it: anger, resentment, confusion, and a vast array of others. This is one of the steep costs of the spiritual life: saying goodbye, letting go, disappointing dear friends and family. It is a heavy burden, one that we must bear without knowing the reasons or ramifications beforehand. Ames endures the loss of a wife and child, alienation from parents, the uncertainty of his family's future, and the intrusion of Jack at the end of his life when he did not have the resources to meet the moment. In other words, his circumstances forced him to play out a script he did not write, and yet he trusts God even while he wrestles with a host of unresolved and conflicting emotions.

For a minister and spiritual pillar of the community, Ames struggles with several negative emotions.[43] Anger overcomes him easily, a family trait, we learn.[44] Resentment, envy, and paranoia are littered throughout the letter, especially paranoia about Jack's potential untoward intentions toward his wife and son.[45] We might expect a reverend nearing the end of his life to display more spiritual equanimity, an unflappable tranquility impervious to the provocations and humiliations of life. Not so. A lifetime of ministry and reflective bent do not preclude or prevent his spiritual shadow side, that is, the spiritually unproductive, maladjusted, and sometimes destructive instincts, sensibilities, characteristics, and reactions of the soul. The shadow side often inverts positive characteristics as their dark mirror image. Ames's sense of justice has anger as its spiritual inverse or shadow side, as it did for his father and grandfather, for instance.

We should not expect spiritual purity or perfection from our religious leaders or from ourselves, for that matter. False perfectionism creates unattainable expectations that only frustrate. If we expect perfect leaders, we will be disappointed. If we expect flawlessness, we will be dismayed, for no soul has ascended to the spiritual summit. We strive without attaining. We pursue without arriving. The long, tortuous spiritual journey teaches us to rely on grace continually. We must differentiate here between the personal and professional implications of spiritual failings. Personally, it calls for grace and rehabilitation. Professionally, however, when spiritual leaders fail—and conspicuous examples abound, sadly—churches and parachurch organizations must take actions to ensure accountability and the safety of their members. Here we focus on how Ames, despite his spiritual maturity in many ways, still struggles with blind spots, mistakes, and miscalculations.

Each stage of the spiritual life presents different challenges and possibilities, as it does chronologically. Youth experience the thrill of an open, exciting future, where they meet the seemingly boundless possibilities of life with idealism and verve. This is how it should be. Young people should dream, they should imagine how their life will unfold, and strive to realize their dreams. Similarly, people new to faith often show tremendous zeal and energy. They want to change the world, to spread the light they have experienced far and wide. Middle age brings realism, often puncturing idealistic bubbles, and the stress and press of weighty responsibilities. Life's disappointments temper expectations, sometimes engendering cynicism. Similarly, as one proceeds spiritually, the realities of the inflexibly of institutions and the cooling of religious fervor sets in, forcing the spiritual person to recalculate their goals and recalibrate their expectations.

Aging entails coming to terms with loss: health, mobility, activity, and, ultimately, life. We naturally resist and recoil, like Ames: "The fact is, I don't want to be old. And I certainly don't want to be dead."[46] Quite the contrary: Ames relishes life, marvels at beauty, and cherishes time with his wife and son. And yet, he knows his time is short, and he worries his son will only remember him in his decrepitude: "How I wish you could have known me in my strength";[47] "I bitterly wish you could know me as a young man."[48] In his prime, Ames was bursting with energy, lucidity, and vitality. In his declining years, his powers naturally diminish, causing Ames frustration and sometimes distress. It also weighs on his much younger wife, Lila: "'Why'd you have to be so damn old.' I ask myself the same question."[49]

Similarly, spiritual advancement brings its own reckonings, including coming to terms with regret, especially moral failings. But it also brings perspective, as we will see.

Physiologically, the effects of old age subject Ames to many minor inconveniences and indignities that annoy, anger, and agitate him. He falls asleep easily.[50] He moves slowly and sometimes wanders off without telling Lila.[51] People worry about him.[52] Jack moves his office downstairs, notably his notebook with its intimate details, including serious concerns and critiques about Jack.[53] All these unwelcome changes underscore his age and highlight his decline. No one, fictional or not, wants to be treated as an invalid, especially while they still feel capable. Socially and professionally, Ames experiences other losses, such as his pastoral power.[54] His old congregation treat him with respect and consideration, but he no longer exerts executive power. Others make the decisions now and for someone accustomed to calling the shots, the loss of operational authority constitutes a significant loss. Ames processes these losses in the letter.

It is hard for caretakers to have the tables turned on them, to become the object of care. Ames bristles at it. It is natural, of course, to lament the loss of health, mobility, and vitality. Spiritually, however, there are opportunities for growth. Old age gives Ames the opportunity to receive grace after a lifetime of giving grace. The economy of grace requires givers and receivers, and givers must learn to be receivers for the system to function.[55] The book of Acts records a teaching of Jesus not found in the Gospels: "It is more blessed to give than receive."[56] In order to bless the givers, the receivers ought to embrace their role in the spiritual transaction. By accepting his new role as the recipient of grace, Ames ironically extends his ministry of blessing to others, even though it involves a role reversal that he does not relish. For the economy of grace to operate, we must be willing to accept a new role as the object of grace.

Spiritual maturity, similarly, involves gains and losses. Ames gains the perspective of age: that life is short, beautiful, and fragile, that we must seize the day. He learns to savor the moments, knowing that they are finite. Facing the end heightens his perceptions and deepens his appreciation. In a sensory celebration of sight and smell, Ames delights in his birthday breakfast: "I woke up this morning to the smell of pancakes, which I dearly love. . . . It is my birthday, so there were marigolds on the table and my stack of pancakes had candles in it."[57] Nothing spectacular, nothing dramatic, just a thoughtful presentation of food and flowers—very mundane at one level. And yet, for Ames, the atmosphere was electric with elation, with the startling reminder of a wife and child in his old age and the appreciation of a special moment together: "I hate to think what I would give for a thousand mornings like this. For two or three."[58] In his awareness of death's approach he teaches us about the preciousness of time.

But Ames also has spiritual blind spots. Most strikingly, he harbors deep resentment and bitterness toward Jack Boughton. He does not welcome him back as a loving godfather, as a loyal friend to his father, or as a minister tasked with emulating the open arms of the father of the Prodigal Son. Instead of embodying grace, he is suspicious, sneaky, and most unbecomingly for a lifelong Christian and clergyperson, unforgiving: "I don't forgive him. I wouldn't know where to begin."[59] For the bulk of the narrative Ames essentially rejects Jack, who reminds him of past pains and intrudes on his attempt at twilight tranquility. He rebuffs his theological questions, giving only stock replies at first, and does not seize on the pastoral opportunities in his return.[60] If he were more spiritually attuned and self-aware, he would realize Jack surfaces his early losses in life and has taken on a more symbolic role in his imagination.

But you cannot love symbols, only people, and by reducing Jack to a symbol of loss, crisis, and suffering he bypasses his authentic spiritual needs. Ames fails Jack for most of the narrative because he does not fully realize his own spiritual underdevelopment, or perhaps devolution, when it comes to Jack. Jack is a blind spot, an instantiation of the limits of his posture of grace, and a cross he refuses to carry. That is, until the end of the story. Ames ultimately adjusts his attitude and embraces his role as a second father to Jack, both a spiritual father and a proxy father for his best friend, who no longer has the capacity to function as a conduit of grace. But for most of the story Ames is paranoid that Jack is angling to steal his wife and child and bewitching him.[61] He brings to every encounter a hermeneutic of suspicion rather than a hermeneutic of grace. Would Jack have stayed in Gilead if Ames had been more receptive to his presence and more helpful?

Spiritual maturity, Ames teaches, does not always happen evenly or steadily. We might grow in some spiritual areas, flounder in others, and regress in still others. We all have blind spots. We all have areas of spiritual underdevelopment, immaturity, and ignorance even if we have reached some spiritual summits. These peaks and valleys are connected, part of the range of our inner spiritual landscape. The years teach Ames to appreciate the sacredness of the ordinary, the beauty of the moment, and the joy of existence. His sins and wounds, however, hobble him in ways he does not fully appreciate, which begins to render him ineffective. Religious leaders, adherents, and spiritual questers are not immune to failure and do not always follow the steady progress model, as we have seen. There are times of rapid growth, times of waiting, and times of regression. We all have areas of strength and weakness. Once we recognize our own spiritual complexity and shortcomings, we can remedy areas of deficiency and lean into areas of strength.

For Ames, the full realization of his role as godfather to Jack and conduit of grace comes after he apologizes for his failure and truly listens to him on his own terms, apart from the anxieties of his own situation. Only then, by practicing selfless presence, can he bless him. Jack comes to Ames's office at the church unannounced and shares with him the secret he could not bring himself to tell his family: he has a wife and child.[62] Of the many complicating factors—Jack's self-sabotaging behavior, her parents' disapproval, and their lack of resources—the most insuperable is her race. Ames notes that she is a "colored woman," and their son is "a light skinned colored boy."[63] The anti-miscegenation laws of the time preclude the legality of their union, so they are forced into surreptitious arrangements that ultimately fail. Jack has come to Gilead to gauge whether they might have a future there. He comes to realize they do not.

That information snaps Ames out of his self-preoccupation and fixation on his own troubles. He still finds himself fumbling, including an ill-advised reference to Jack's deceased daughter, but he continues in the conversation to try to offer sound advice.[64] Would his father accept the situation? Could they make a life in Gilead? Ames could not say with certainty, but he promises to reflect on the matter. Although their conversation is strained and they trade barbed comments, they stumble toward a mutual understanding. They are both in unconventional family situations. They have both lost a daughter. They both face the loss of their current families: Jack through societal barriers and Ames through his failing health. And yet, in the sharing of their wounds and in Jack's willingness to trust Ames with his secret, Ames begins to embrace his role as Jack's second father, even though the prospects of a life in Gilead seem dim.[65]

In the end, Jack loses hope and leaves town: "Jack is leaving. Glory is so upset with him that she came to talk to me about it."[66] As he walks toward the bus stop, Ames spots him and calls him over. He wants to sit with him in his desolation, share in his misery, states of mind he knows intimately. Beyond solidarity, however, Ames wants to send Jack away not with Glory's understandable exasperation—"This is it. This is your masterpiece"[67]—but with a blessing: "The thing I would like, actually, is to bless you."[68] Jack consents, lowers his head, upon which Ames places his aged hand and bestows the Aaronic blessing, followed by a prayer: "Lord, bless John Ames Boughton, this beloved son and brother and husband and father."[69] It is the spiritual and emotional climax of the novel and, in fact, of the entire Gilead series. Ames completes and fulfils his vocation by becoming the father to *his* Prodigal Son after failing him since his return.

Ames sees the episode as the culmination of his humble ministry in a small town: "In fact I'd have gone through seminary and ordination and all the years intervening for that one moment."[70] It puts him back into alignment with his default posture of grace, which has been bent out of shape since his return. As the letter proceeds, his hostile preoccupation with Jack's long history of hijinks and hurt grows, a clear signal of his spiritual misalignment. At the end, when Jack unburdens himself with him, Ames finally hears it with pastoral benevolence, and thus returns to himself as an embodiment of grace. This liberates him. Ames's bus-stop blessing of Jack enables him to embrace the meanings and motivations that define his life, and their total sufficiency, even at death: "There are a thousand thousand reasons to live this life, every one of them sufficient."[71] It was a long road, with many detours, but Ames finally reaches his spiritual destination: grace.

For those engaged in ministry, or spiritual mentorship, the departing blessing contains several key insights. First, self-knowledge is essential, particularly the realization of the reality of blind spots. It is always easier to see the faults in others than in ourselves. As the term indicates, it can be hard to see or admit to our spiritual deficiencies, but with the help of friends and family willing to give honest assessments, we can begin to identify areas to improve. Only then, under the light of self-directed scrutiny, can we begin to see ourselves as equally faulty and in need of grace. In other words, we are works in progress—souls under construction. As Ames slowly comes to terms with his anger, self-deception, and bitterness he becomes better able to administer grace to Jack. Too often, however, religious leaders and ardent practitioners feign unimpeachability, to the detriment of themselves *and* those they serve.

Second, spiritual conversations do not always start or go smoothly, as the conversations between Jack and Ames illustrate. Before the blessing, during the discussion of the doctrine of predestination, the conversation falters for many reasons.[72] It was probably the wrong time and place. Jack does not relent despite Ames's reluctance and Glory's warning. Ames does not perceive the personal nature of the question for Jack, nor his sincerity, so he keeps him at arm's length. Similar obstacles of suspicions, unstated motives, and misunderstanding plague later talks. If Ames had heard the need behind the question and even Jack's hostility, he could have responded better. If Jack had chosen a better time and place and prefaced the discussion better, Ames might have been more helpful. We must read the spiritual subtexts, hear what people are trying to say rather than what they are saying, and discern the right moments for delicate and difficult theological and spiritual conversations.

Third, defining spiritual moments come when we least expect them. Whereas the spiritual life involves intentional practices, concentrated effort, and orchestrated events, the outcomes do not follow a script. It is not a blueprint for sublime bliss; it is a life open to transcendence. If we try to manufacture a spiritual moment, it will often come up empty or, even worse, backfire. Ames might have hoped for a profound spiritual moment with his friend Old Boughton or with his wife or child: perhaps a shared experience or theological realization or spiritual breakthrough. Instead, life presents him with Jack in an existential freefall while Ames suffers declining health. It is not the ending Ames would have wished for at the start of the letter, but he comes to accept it as *his* ending and as beautiful in its brokenness. He finally learns the hard-won lessons of spiritual maturity: gratitude for life, openness to the inroads of grace in unexpected places, and surrender to mystery.

Conclusion

Gilead sparkles with spiritual insight. Readers find themselves aglow in grace, absorbed in the beauty of the characters as they face their respective crises. Suffering and celebration are interwoven into the fabric of the narrative, creating an irresolvable interplay that invites a spirituality of wonder and grace.[73] At one level, it is a story about suffering: Ames dies, Jack leaves town, and Lila and her son are left in limbo. It underscores the indignity and inevitability of suffering, as well as the ways we attempt to ameliorate it or at least endure it with dignity and hopefulness. At another level, it is a story about celebration: an ode to the beauty of the world, a poem for the brokenhearted, a song of grace. It explores the depth dimensions of existence, where we seek to discover our "reason" and bask in the endless mysteries of love, beauty, and grace. *Gilead* expands our spiritual imagination, reigniting our sense of wonder and awakening our empathy toward those in the throes of suffering.

The sea-light that birthed *Gilead* never fades for its devoted readers, even after Ames's light extinguishes. It shimmers in their souls, stretching to new horizons as it finds new generations of readers. The origin of the story itself teaches a valuable final lesson. Robinson might have felt very frustrated with her disrupted Christmas plans. Instead of brooding, however, she embraced her environment, and took advantage of the opportunity to attend to something magical gestating in her imagination. The spiritual life is often like that. Best laid plans go awry, and we face a choice: bemoan or discover. Hidden in these moments of unexpected delay or problems or crises lie gems that await our discovery. We cannot find them if we fixate on the loss. We can only discover them if we remember that these unwelcome moments contain golden opportunities to the spiritually alert. So the next time our plans fail, after the initial disappointment subsides, let us ask: "What is the spiritual opportunity in this?"

Notes

1 Sarah Fay, "Marilynne Robinson: The Art of Fiction no. 198," *Paris Review* 186 (2008), https://www.theparisreview.org/interviews/5863/the-art-of-fiction-no-198-marilynne-robinson.
2 Marilynne Robinson, talk given at the 2012 National Book Festival, https://www.loc.gov/item/webcast-5654/.
3 Engebretson, *Understanding Marilynne Robinson*, 35.
4 See their two-part conversation in *The New York Review of Books*, November 5, 2015, http://www.nybooks.com/articles/2015/11/05/president-obama-marilynne-robinson-conversation/ and November 19, 2015, http://www.nybooks.com/articles/2015/11/19/president-obama-marilynne-robinson-conversation-2/.
5 Marilynne Robinson, *Gilead* (New York: Farrar, Straus & Giroux, 2004), 3.
6 Robinson, *Gilead*, 247.
7 Robinson, *Gilead*, 14, 71. "I have seen moonlight strong enough to cast shadows any number of times." Robinson, *Gilead*, 74.
8 Robinson, *Gilead*, 14. Robinson bases this powerful aesthetic and spiritual episode in the novel on a personal experience: "And I did once see the sun set as a full moon rose, something I never will forget." Marilynne Robinson, quoted in Scott Hoezee, "A World of Beautiful Souls: An Interview with Marilynne Robinson," *The Reformed Journal*, May 16, 2005, https://reformedjournal.com/a-world-of-beautiful-souls-an-interview-with-marilynne-robinson/.
9 Robinson, *Gilead*, 53.
10 Robinson, *Gilead*, 52.
11 Robinson, *Gilead*, 65.
12 Robinson, *Gilead*, 141.
13 Robinson, *Gilead*, 94.
14 Robinson, *Gilead*, 94–96.
15 Robinson, *Gilead*, 96.
16 Robinson, *Gilead*, 95.
17 Robinson, *Gilead*, 114.
18 Robinson, *Gilead*, 102. "Grief itself has often returned me to that morning, when I took communion from my father's hand. I remember it as communion, and I believe that's what it was" (96).
19 Robinson, *Gilead*, 95.

20 For more on how this scene in the novel illustrates the surprising ways beauty transforms times of turmoil and hardship, especially its redemptive and eschatological significance, see, Mark S. M. Scott, "Beauty from Ashes: Aesthetic Transformations of Suffering in *Gilead*," *CRUX* 52, no. 3/4 (2016): 11–18.
21 Robinson, *Gilead*, 71.
22 Augustine, *The Confessions*, 2nd ed., trans. Maria Boulding, ed. John E. Rotelle (New York: New City Press, 2012), I.7.12, p. 47; II.6.12, p. 70; VII.17.23, p. 176; X.27.38, p. 262.
23 Robinson, *Gilead*, 9, 185.
24 Robinson, *Gilead*, 9.
25 Robinson, *Gilead*, 247.
26 Robinson, *Gilead*, 115.
27 Robinson, *Gilead*, 54.
28 Robinson, *Gilead*, 28.
29 Robinson, *Gilead*, 24.
30 Robinson, *Gilead*, 26. "As I have told you, I was the good son, so to speak, the one who never left his father's house—even when his father did, a fact which surely puts my credentials beyond all challenge." Robinson, *Gilead*, 238.
31 Robinson, *Gilead*, 234.
32 Robinson, *Gilead*, 17, 24, 65.
33 Robinson, *Gilead*, 63.
34 Robinson, *Gilead*, 64.
35 Robinson, *Gilead*, 101.
36 Robinson, *Gilead*, 26.
37 Robinson, *Gilead*, 9, 102, 133–34, 202.
38 Robinson, *Gilead*, 6.
39 Robinson, *Gilead*, 39.
40 Psalm 90:12.
41 Robinson, *Gilead*, 9, 238–39.
42 Robinson, *Gilead*, 131.
43 Robinson, *Gilead*, 164, 188, 190.
44 Robinson, *Gilead*, 34, 84–85.
45 Robinson, *Gilead*, 125, 141.
46 Robinson, *Gilead*, 141.
47 Robinson, *Gilead*, 94.
48 Robinson, *Gilead*, 141.
49 Robinson, *Gilead*, 50.

50 Robinson, *Gilead*, 126, 199.
51 Robinson, *Gilead*, 73.
52 Robinson, *Gilead*, 74.
53 Robinson, *Gilead*, 128, 213.
54 Robinson, *Gilead*, 110.
55 Old Boughton expresses the dual dynamic of the economy of grace to Jack and Teddy, using himself as an example to protect Jack's dignity: "Part of it is giving care and another part is accepting it. The second part is difficult and very important. . . . So I want you boys to promise me you will help each other." Robinson, *Home*, 261.
56 Acts 20:35.
57 Robinson, *Gilead*, 50.
58 Robinson, *Gilead*, 50.
59 Robinson, *Gilead*, 164.
60 Robinson, *Gilead*, 150.
61 Robinson, *Gilead*, 128, 131, 141, 180–81, 214.
62 Robinson, *Gilead*, 217.
63 Robinson, *Gilead*, 219.
64 Robinson, *Gilead*, 230–31.
65 Robinson, *Gilead*, 231–32.
66 Robinson, *Gilead*, 237.
67 Robinson, *Gilead*, 240.
68 Robinson, *Gilead*, 241.
69 Robinson, *Gilead*, 241.
70 Robinson, *Gilead*, 242.
71 Robinson, *Gilead*, 243.
72 Robinson, *Gilead*, 149–53.
73 Robinson, *Gilead*, 71.

5

Wounded Souls in *Home*

But the soul finds its own home
if it ever has a home at all.
—Marilynne Robinson, *Home*

Published four years after *Gilead* (2004), *Home* (2008) stands as a "co-quel" to its Pulitzer Prize–winning predecessor.[1] Set at the same time and place as *Gilead*, *Home* shifts the focus away from the Ames to the Boughton family, and specifically from Reverend Ames's viewpoint to Glory Boughton's. While both novels have their own independent integrity, they clearly belong together thematically and theologically, even whilst they retain their distinctive valences and aesthetics. *Home* has its own inner complexity, as A. O. Scott captures well in a review: "It is at once hard and forgiving, bitter and joyful, fanatical and serene. It is a wild, eccentric, radical work of literature."[2] As always, Robinson defies convention, boldly and unapologetically following her own intuitions and sensibilities, inviting her readers to see Gilead in a new light by homing in on the tense interplay between three wounded souls in the Boughton home.

Home did not receive the same thunderous critical recognition as *Gilead*, although it was nominated for the National Book Award and won the Orange Prize for Fiction, awarded to "the best Anglophone novel by a female author."[3] In contrast to the first-person narration of *Gilead*, *Home* employs third-person narration.[4] Glory becomes the "focalizing consciousness" of the novel, which foregrounds her altruistic care for her "aged father and alcoholic brother" but backgrounds her "personal history and emotion."[5] Once again, readers must ask themselves about the reliability of her narration. As Ames carefully curates his account of his life, sometimes sanctimoniously, so Glory accents Jack's winsome qualities and overlooks or downplays his worst in her hermeneutic of generosity and protectiveness.[6] For both novels, then, readers must read between the lines, given the selective slant and hidden agendas of the narrators. Nothing should be taken at face value in Robinson's novels.

Robinson's attentiveness to the distinctive soul-shape of her characters, even or perhaps especially at the level of narration, aligns with her emphasis on the irreducible uniqueness of consciousness and its capacity for brilliance, distortion, and self-deception. *Home* highlights these themes well through its perspectival shifts. When it relays an incident also found in *Gilead*, significant differences sometimes arise.[7] These differences force the reader to wonder which rendering is more reliable as a whole and in its details, and why. The simultaneity of the novels, combined with the perspectival shift, raises interesting questions about how different characters experience the same situation differently. *Home* portrays Ames in a less saintly light than *Gilead*. Glory becomes more three-dimensional in *Home*. Jack, while troubled and problematic in both novels, is more sympathetic in the latter than the former. These tensions signal the subjectivity of experience and perception.

Home centers on the return of Jack Boughton to his family home after a twenty-year absence.[8] His unexpected return stirs his elderly father out of his twilight abstractions and back into the cares of the world. It also activates Glory, who becomes a caretaker for both her aging father and her wayward brother despite her own internal crises. For the duration of the story Jack seeks to find his way back to himself, helping around the house, caring for his father, and talking with Glory. Glory tries her best to make the house hospitable for him while also attending to her father as he slides into the incapacitations of old age. Finally, Old Boughton tries to extend grace to his estranged son, but ultimately fails. The plaintive polyphony that plays throughout the novel strikes chords of joy and sadness, hope and despair, beauty and brokenness. *Home* tenderly and touchingly witnesses the fraught dynamic of three wounded souls trying to care for each other under adverse conditions. They fail, but their effort reveals the tenacity of their love.

Glory's return to Gilead prompts excitement from her father, the opening words of the novel: "'Home to stay, Glory! Yes!'"[9] Boughton's exhilaration overcompensates for his sadness. He knows her homecoming comes at the cost of some hope, some dream, some joy unattained. He does not pry or push her for details on the circumstances that bring her home, respecting her privacy and genuinely pleased by her return. But Glory's state of crisis is expressed immediately by the omniscient narrator: "Dear God, she thought, Dear God in heaven. So began and ended all her prayers these days, which were really cries of amazement."[10] Slowly the novel unveils the reasons for her return. She gave her trusting heart to an untrustworthy man, to a married man, in fact.[11] Her memories sanitize and spin the embarrassing, bizarre romance.[12] She can barely admit to herself that she was the target of a romantic con job.[13]

Jack's return also signals some doom, in keeping with the general tenor of his existence. From childhood to early adulthood, Jack's problems grew increasingly serious, culminating in impregnating a poor neighborhood girl, Annie Wheeler, whose daughter eventually dies.[14] Soon thereafter Jack disappears from the family, fading into memory, even as his brother Teddy tries to locate him in St. Louis from time to time.[15] Jack's call to the family home comes out of the blue and as a shock. They do not know where he has been or what he has been doing, so when he asks to visit, some misfortune lies behind it. After a couple of false starts, Jack eventually appears on the back doorstep disheveled and drunk.[16] For the next few months, Jack slowly reveals aspects of his crisis to Glory as he reacquaints himself with her and gradually learns to trust her, but he never shares the full scope of his situation: he wants to find a way to reunite with his wife and son.[17]

Boughton similarly finds himself in an unexpected time of crisis. Physically, he is in a state of decline, unable to perform many of the basic tasks of life anymore, and unable to stay awake for very long. The deterioration of age hobbles him in other ways, however. Spiritually, he finds it difficult to exhibit the kind of grace he has always wished to extend to his lost son. The years of waiting and worrying have taken a toll on him emotionally, so when Jack finally returns, he cannot sustain his welcome.[18] At the end of the story, he withdraws his hand from Jack's extended hand and turns away: "'Tired of it!' he said."[19] In a dramatic reversal of the parable of the prodigal son, the father turns away from the son, refusing welcome. Boughton falters when his son needed him most, failing to realize his dream of welcoming him home with open arms. *Home*, then, depicts the intersection of three characters in crisis seeking solace with each other.

Spiritually, times of crisis often drive people home. Sometimes, as in *Home*, they return to their family home to heal from failed relationships (Glory) or to regroup from setbacks (Jack). The family home represents safety and shelter from the storms of life, and as a time capsule of childhood memories it helps to ground and reorient in times of upheaval. There are other ways of homecoming, however. We might return to family and friends who have been formative to us, from whom we may have drifted over the years. We return to them as an emotional homecoming, where we return to ourselves through their warmth and wisdom. People, rather than places, can be our home: they help us to feel at home in the world. Homecoming might mean, for others, a return to healthy habits from which they have strayed, such as prayer and Bible reading. Crises destabilize, thereby initiating stabilizing countermeasures to find balance and direction.

"What does it mean to come home?," Glory wonders.[20] In the first place, homecomings are relationally, emotionally, and spiritually complex. Once home, we recall the good *and* bad memories and realize how they shaped us positively and negatively. Some enjoyed happy childhoods; others endured difficult ones or worse. For most, however, it is more of a mixed bag of good and bad, formative and deformative. Life rarely gives pure, undiluted moments of happiness, even in childhood. Away from home, we can easily forget or shelve these memories, but in the family home the memories flood back. We can only bask in the glow of the good memories if we resolve the experience of the bad. That takes time and effort, sometimes with the help of a skilled counsellor or therapist. If we come home in an unsettled state, the return can further unsettle us unless we come to terms with the painful memories.

Another difficulty of homecoming is regression. Have you ever noticed that when you return home for the holidays or a family event you behave differently than in your everyday life? We find ourselves playing out old scripts of behavior with our parents and siblings, sliding back into old roles and reliving old conflicts. The habitual pull toward regression is hard to resist once we walk through the front door (or, in Jack's case, the back). It is impossible to resist if we are unaware of it, given the years of conditioning involved. Without even realizing it, our family maneuvers us into old, familiar roles, and we probably unconsciously do the same with them. This is natural and not necessarily pernicious, but when it prevents us from entering new stages, it must be identified, resisted, and rejected. If we operate in the old paradigms, new positive family dynamics cannot arise. If we stay in the old roles of our childhood self, the adult self cannot emerge.

Coming home, then, does not guarantee instant healing. In fact, it can compound the pain if we arrive unaware of the emotional and behavioral complexities involved. In *Home*, Old Boughton regresses to the chiding father with Jack more than once. He checks his language and asks him if he was responsible for some local mischief, like when he was a boy.[21] Glory slides back into her role as the caregiver and peacemaker of the family, always trying to ensure everyone's getting along and comfortable, often at her own expense. Jack, for his part, reverts to many of his old ways, including poking fun at Glory, worrying and provoking his father, and absconding from the family, hiding in the loft.[22]

As they play out their well-worn roles, old memories and feelings bubble to the surface, engendering conflicts that delay growth and prevent healing. Only when they abandon the theater of replaying old family roles and interact as their current selves, with their respective wounds, do they begin to encounter each other, sometimes in healing ways.

Similarly, the same complex dynamics of mixed memories, tensions, and regression operate interpersonally with friends and family outside of the family home. In times of crisis, we may go to them for healing, but they have changed, and so have we, so it might not have the salubrious effect that we had hoped for. That does not mean that they have failed us or that we no longer have a relational home, that we are interpersonally isolated or emotionally orphaned. It might mean, rather, that we must establish new dynamics—new relational pathways—for something new and life-giving to arise. Or it might be an invitation to find new ways to return home to the self, either through new relationships, or new habits, or new frames of mind. Despite his best efforts, Jack ultimately fails to renegotiate his relationship with his family home and his sister and father, and that is in part because he could not move past the old memories and dysfunctions.

Even though they could not save each other from their respective plights, they were able to enjoy moments of respite. They found some solace and partial healing in the predictable rhythms they developed during his stay. Jack would help his father. Glory would make coffee. They would eat simple meals together. These small acts of kindness and hospitality conveyed grace. It gave them the semblance of normalcy, enabling them to manufacture a sense of family after losing their dreams of family in different ways. The diurnal rhythms of domesticity temporarily dulled their pain over lost love, lost time, lost family, and the loss of vitality and hope. Their time together, then, was not a total failure in the final analysis. It was an interlude that created space and time for them to try to come to terms with their situations and seek new ways to navigate unwelcome realities. There were happy moments, times of refreshment, and even joy.

Their unrealistic and idealistic goals undercut their noble efforts, however. Glory tries to stabilize Jack, care for her father, and find a new life in Gilead, perhaps as a teacher, regardless of the obstacles to all three objectives. Jack tries to find his footing back home in a desperate attempt to provide a life for his wife and son, despite the odds against him. Old Boughton tries to recreate the reunion of the father with the Prodigal Son in Luke 15:11–32 in his own home, failing to realize that his advanced age and Jack's persistent prodigality would make that impossible. These were admirable, sincere, well-intentioned goals fueled more by desperation and hope than a realistic assessment of the situation. They were doomed from the outset because they ignored the practical challenges they faced and the spiritual landscape they inhabited.

Realism means neither the abandonment of hope nor the abdication of dreams. We must hope against hope, we must dream new realities into existence. Realism means that we set goals in the context of the world we find ourselves in, rather than in the world we wished we lived in. If, in a spiritual crisis, we return home in search of healing, we will likely be disappointed because we have not considered the limitations of our family, friends, and environment, or the barriers *we* bring to the healing process. Healing takes time: there are no short-cuts or magical solutions to problems that have festered for years. Instead, it is more prudent to set achievable goals: rest, renewal, revisioning. If Jack had returned to Gilead with the hope of saying goodbye to his father, apologizing for the pain he brought to his family, and to reconnect with Glory, it would have been a more productive visit. He would have been less likely to slide into the despair that led him to attempt suicide.

Similarly, if Glory had returned home without assuming the entire weight of caretaking for her frail father and floundering brother, she might have been able to use the time more as an opportunity to process the vicissitudes of life, assist her family in a more limited role, and chart a new path forward, probably away from Gilead. For his part, Old Boughton, desperately desiring to extend the open arms of the father to Jack, also set his expectations of himself and for the situation too high. A lifetime of waiting and longing for Jack had attenuated his spiritual strength, so it was unrealistic to think he could sustain a posture of grace in the face of Jack's actual troubled presence. If he had simply tried to reconnect with him, appreciate what Jack could give rather than what he wanted from him, and enjoy the time as an unexpected visit rather than as a theologically and emotionally loaded "return," it might have been less onerous for him.

When we return home, either physically, emotionally, or spiritually, let us begin with setting reasonable, achievable goals. See the return as a respite from the crisis or turmoil that prompted it. See it as a time to reset and gain perspective before a major decision or major event. See it as an opportunity to reconnect with family, friends, and, ultimately, ourselves through intentional introspection and interpersonal engagement. See it as a time to recover without falling into the trap of expecting complete healing, support, perspective, peace, or any other idealistic, unreasonable goal. Unrealistic expectations will set us back if we pin our hopes to them. Let us think more about our attitude than about our objectives. If we walk through the front door with an open heart—an openness to discovery, correction, and connection—we may find that what we receive will be better than what we had anticipated at the outset. Let us cultivate a spirit of receptivity.

At the same time, we must not slide into the myopia of therapeutic self-centeredness. Despite our urgent needs and low capacities in these moments, we still have something to give, however small it might seem to us. As we cultivate receptivity, we must also find ways to give, to enrich the lives of others. Make it a priority. As we focus on the needs of others, we become less fixated on ourselves and our problems, which alleviates some of the pressure. Also, in the process of giving, we might find or rediscover aspects of ourselves that might be a partial salve or a solution to the pain or problems that afflict us. Ironically, by turning the focus away from ourselves to others, we simultaneously help both, like when Jack helped around the house, commiserated with Glory, and assisted his father. "I'm so tired of myself," Jack says to Glory in tears as she cuts his hair.[23] Decentering enables recentering. Giving facilitates receiving.

In the end, every wounded soul must take responsibility for their own actions, their own road to healing and wholeness. It is not up to anyone else to heal us. Nor is it even possible. As Glory says with Jack in mind: "But the soul finds its own home if it ever has a home at all."[24] And that is as true for Glory as it is for Jack as it is for us. We can feel so powerless, so impotent to change our circumstances. Never trust those feelings of resignation, abdication, and despair. We can make new decisions, slight adjustments, that can fundamentally alter our reality. It takes time, sacrifice, and intentionality. Of course, we are still at the whim of forces, people, and situations we cannot control. That has always been the site of transformational agency: exercising freedom amid a myriad of constraints. The focus should not be on the constraints but on our ability to maneuver within those constraints, and perhaps our ability to free ourselves from them ultimately.

Obviously Old Boughton could not alter his advanced age, with its cognitive, physical, and emotional impairments. Though hobbled by time and worry, he still welcomes Jack home enthusiastically and offers a prayer of welcome.[25] For most of Jack's visit he was able to extend the open arms of grace, even if he tired at the end.[26] In a similar vein, Glory could not change her past relationship, nor its embarrassment, nor the awkward situation it left her in. Yet, even in her disillusionment and uncertainty, she offers love, wisdom, and support to her father and brother. Likewise, Jack, though at odds with himself and society, and suffering the consequences of a lifetime of irresponsibility, still tenderly cares for his father and sister in a variety of thoughtful ways. He did not only receive their love, care, and attention, he gave to them from his limited reservoir. Wounded souls can still give. Wounded souls are more than their wounds. Wounded souls are still beautiful, still able to shine their light, however dimmed.

Finding beauty in brokenness subverts the specious association of beauty with youth, health, popularity, and success. Since these all pass away, true beauty must lie beyond the superficial and ephemeral. On the surface Jack, Glory, and their father do not exhibit the standard hallmarks of beauty, so we have to look deeper to see how beauty breaks through their brokenness. The same applies to us. To locate the deeper sites of beauty, we must first acknowledge and accept the wounds, which we naturally conceal. For instance, we often hide physical injuries and ailments, sometimes without knowing the reason. Perhaps we do not want the sympathy or attention it draws, or perhaps we do not want to face our mortality, or perhaps we want to feel normal again, even only momentarily. Correspondingly, we also hide our emotional and spiritual wounds, fearing judgment, rejection, and misunderstanding. These protective mechanisms, fueled by a combination of self-preservation and self-consciousness, are very natural.

Natural, yes, but ultimately misguided and destructive. With physical wounds, injuries, and illness, concealment delays treatment, which prolongs and worsens the condition. An infection, left untreated, will fester. A broken bone unset will misalign. A disease ignored will spread. Many people have died prematurely by refusing to seek medical help for these problems. Similarly, emotional and spiritual ailments worsen and spread if left undiagnosed and untreated. Rather than conceal, deny, and isolate, it is wiser to bring them into the healing light of others, despite the possible unpleasantness or embarrassment. Revealing problems opens the possibility of amelioration. Even if some wounds never fully heal, at least you will have a community of support to journey with you in your brokenness. The Boughton household, accustomed to secrecy around Jack since childhood, settled into a pattern of concealment that prevented the healing power of transparency and treatment.

Granting the cathartic value of sharing still leaves the practical question: Who should we trust with our wounds? Who should we admit into the inner sanctum of our suffering? It is sacred ground, and not all are equally trustworthy. Not all are equally helpful, insightful, or available. Not all have earned the right to hear our story in all its complexity, to enter the intimacy of shared pain. If we have been hurt before, especially by someone in a position of spiritual trust—a parent, teacher, or clergyperson, for instance—it will be almost impossible to take the leap without therapeutic intervention. Exposing our emotional and spiritual wounds entails vulnerability; it subjects us to further wounds if mishandled, and it is easily mishandled. Too often people filter other people's stories through the prism of their own experience and respond with advice that suits their own personality and situation, not that of the other person. Deep listening requires suspending our sensibilities and backgrounding our problems to hear clearly what the hurting person is saying *on their terms*.

This, of course, is what Ames fails to do at first with Jack. He is so consumed with his own crises, so embittered by Jack's past, so caught up in his own affairs that he does not make room for Jack's story, does not create an atmosphere conducive to him sharing his turmoil. Outwardly, Ames exhibits the kindness befitting his role as a clergyman and godfather, but inwardly he seethes with distrust, resentment, and bitterness. His inner hostility seeps through without him realizing it. When Jack comes to his church during a Sunday service, rather than capitalizing on the opportunity to extend grace and welcome, he passive-aggressively attacks him from the pulpit with homiletical hostility.[27] When Jack later confides in him, Ames begins with a clumsy and hurtful reference to his deceased child, probably another involuntary eruption of his embittered consciousness toward Jack.[28] Ames is not ready to hear him or to help at first.

As we have seen, *Home* sees these events through the lens of the Boughton household. When the same scene plays out in both novels, instructive differences emerge. For instance, in *Gilead*, Ames tells the story of Jack's visit to his church through his sanitized point of view. He begins with the innocuous observation that he strayed from his scriptural text in his sermon, only to later reveal that Jack attended the service: a momentous spiritual event for both families.[29] After all, Ames was chosen by Old Boughton to be "the father of his soul," a soul that rarely darkened the doors of Gilead's churches.[30] Clearly Ames has struggled to live up to that role, and Jack's return to town has been unwelcome to him, even as he recognizes its redemptive possibilities. In fact, for most of *Gilead* Ames wrestles with his feelings of hostility and resentment toward his godson.

Jack's presence startles and unsettles Ames in *Gilead*: "Then young Boughton came to the service. That was nothing I would have expected. . . . Your mother looked at him to say good morning, and then she did not look at him again. Not once."[31] Immediately Ames's suspicions and paranoia arise and put him in a self-centered, defensive state of mind. By allowing his hostilities toward Jack to fester internally, he now loses the ability to restrain himself when the pivotal moment arrives. Old Boughton dreamt of the moment when Ames would give a sermon of grace to his son, to sound notes of welcome and hope. Genesis 21, which tells the story of the deliverance of Hagar and Ishmael from the ravages of the desert, offers obvious soteriological implications and applications that Ames ignores in favor Genesis 22, the sacrifice of Isaac, which has problematic implications and associations for Jack, more than Ames even realizes at the time.[32]

Ames fails in a crucial moment, and in *Gilead* he strains to clarify his pastoral intentions for several paragraphs, but to no avail. His exegetical excursions sound spiritual, but they evade the real point, mainly from himself: Ames refuses to welcome Jack home, refuses to embrace him as his spiritual son, and thereby withholds grace. But he cannot really admit the failure to himself yet. He downplays his hostility. In fact, he spiritualizes it. And he offers excuses: he was tired, he was taken off guard, he was well intentioned. "Your mother looked anxious."[33] Lila instantly realizes his misstep, while Ames once again looks at his wife and godson with eyes of suspicion: "It did strike me as strange that she didn't look at him even one time."[34] The moment was lost and the point of Sunday morning church—embedded in the term itself, "service"—was missed because he was not ready to serve.

Later, after some sleepless nights and soul-searching, Ames recognizes his mistake. Clergy are not immune to self-deception, of course, but Ames is too self-aware and self-critical to stay deceived for long. "The truth is, as I stood there in the pulpit, looking down on the three of you, you looked to me like a handsome young family, and my evil old heart rose within me . . ." Finally, Ames perceives the truth he has studiously avoided: "the old covetise I have mentioned elsewhere came over me, and I felt the way I used to feel when the beauty of other lives was a misery and offense to me. And I felt as if I were looking back from the grave."[35] Ames facilitates his own spiritual breakthrough, but only after some extensive self-deception and self-evasion. Afterwards, he seeks to make amends indirectly through an unannounced visit and some small talk, but the damage has been done.[36]

Home, however, does not downplay or gloss over the severity of the event. Whereas in *Gilead* it is a troubling bit of self-realization, in *Home* it is a betrayal: "Her father had suffered a terrible shock. It was his habit to consider Ames another self, for most purposes. And here his son, for whose spiritual comfort and peace he had prayed endlessly . . . his son had made himself vulnerable to him and had been injured, insulted."[37] Jack went to Ames's church with honest intentions, purposively and almost hopefully, only to be crushed. "Ah, little sister, these old fellows play rough."[38] He then relays the injury: "But the worst of it he wasn't even speaking from notes, Glory. The old devil was extemporizing. Very effectively, I might add, for a man of his age."[39] Jack felt targeted, humiliated, and essentially run out of church. "I'll never forgive him," Glory vows afterwards.[40] Twice, actually.[41] It only fuels his despair and prompts his departure from town.

The incident causes a temporary fissure, maybe even a breach, between lifelong friends. In the immediate aftermath Old Boughton was inconsolable and unforgiving. When the telephone rang he would snarl: "If it's Ames, tell him I'm dead."[42] Jack was the deep, lifelong wound of his father, the wound Ames was meant to help tend, perhaps even mend in some way. "Who better than Jack's second father, his father's second self, to say the words of welcome and comfort he could not say? It would never have occurred to him that Ames would not speak to the boy as if from his own heart."[43] The severity of Ames's failure as a friend, pastor, and godfather, masked and mitigated in *Gilead*, is starkly displayed in *Home*. What follows are days of mourning, then small gestures of peace and reconciliation, initiated, ironically from the offended party, Jack.[44]

This story, as well as the conversation on predestination soon afterwards in both narratives, demonstrates the perspectival nature of human experience and memory. Here, in the same incident, we see multiple perspectives collide. At first Ames sees it as a regrettable miscue, but later recognizes the hidden hostility behind it. Lila seems to see it as an unfounded expression of insecurity and perhaps melancholy, judging by her reaction during the service and afterwards. Jack sees it as a direct attack, but later works toward reconciliation. Old Boughton and Glory see it as a shocking betrayal, unforgivable if not for the Christian imperative to forgive all the same. The same incident yields multiple perspectives, interpretations, and reactions, many of them contradictory.

There are more than two sides to every story. In fact, there are almost endless ways to interpret events, especially when they are emotionally laden, and every person might see things in multiple ways, as Ames eventually does. When we know that situations can be seen from contrasting vantage points, we realize the difficulty of capturing exactly "what happened" because the event meant different things to different participants. To try to dissect what it meant to each person and how that relates to their context, sensibilities, and experiences opens paths for empathy. Ames, tired, sick, and under stress, lashed out without fully realizing it at the time. Jack, highly sensitive, perhaps overinterpreted the hostility of Ames's sermon and overreacted to it when talking with Glory. Glory and Old Boughton, so concerned for Jack, so invested in his spiritual welfare, failed to remember Ames's impediments. In other words, we see the same event differently because we come to it from different places and react to it from within those contexts.

This does not entail a solipsistic or subjective metaphysics whereby we reduce the universe to our singular perspective. Perspectival multiplicity denies neither the possibility of objective truth nor the validity of other viewpoints. We know the bare facts of many of these encounters. Instead, it prompts us to remember the mediated nature of human experience. We experience the world as the souls we are, with the totality of our experiences, capacities, sensibilities, proclivities, and blind spots. So do all other souls. The same "event" can mean different things to different souls precisely because we all inhabit the same world slightly differently, sometimes dramatically differently. We all have a unique soulprint—a spiritual and existential distinctiveness—that shapes our reality. Hence, we can affirm the validity of multiple vantage points or subjective experiences without denying objective facts and realities.

When conflict arises, then, we can navigate it more ably. We can say: "No, they didn't say that—those exact words—but you took what they said as an attack." Ames did not say: "Jack Boughton, the notorious sinner in the first pew. The gasoline-scented fellow."[45] Jack, shaped by a persistent sense of spiritual exile, took Ames's words as personally directed. And they were, but perhaps not as spiteful as he supposed, though more spiteful than Ames suspected. What Glory and Old Boughton took as betrayal was more the outcome of exhaustion, frustration, and spiritual wrestling. Disentangling the different threads of knotty conflicts highlights how easily entwined souls get twisted up in themselves and others. The ability to see the different narratives at play creates the possibility of peace and reconciliation.

But when helpers hurt, the wound cuts deeper. Unfortunately, we live in a world where people commissioned with the care of souls abuse their vocation and betray the trust of those under their spiritual guidance. Sadly, this is all too common. Wolves conceal themselves in shepherd's clothing, preying on the innocent. We must be vigilant to expose and stop them. Here, however, I want to touch on unmalicious pastoral failure rather than clergy abuse. When people in pastoral care let us down, as Ames let Jack down, it compounds the wounds we already carry. If a clergy person is unwilling or unable to assist us in our spiritual journey, then we should turn elsewhere for spiritual guidance. It is easy to become disillusioned about organized religion and religious people in those moments, but we must always remember that clergy are just as flawed as the rest of us and that a host of mitigating factors, including personalities, sensibilities, and expectations, can impede spiritual care.

Ames simply was in no position to offer spiritual guidance, given his declining health.[46] It was natural for Jack to ask for help, but he, like his father, was too diminished physically and emotionally to offer the kind of care Jack needed. In a sense, neither are to blame for the pastoral failure: Ames's ailments and Jack's struggles were not fully known to either. Both were flying in the dark. Once it became apparent, Jack rightly withdrew and Ames rightly redoubled his efforts, finding his form at the end with the bench blessing. Like Jack, many people have had bad experiences in church that dissuade them from returning. That is a natural reaction to being hurt and disappointed. In those moments, we should remember not to universalize our bad experience and to be open to new experiences in new church environments when we are ready. We might find a new community of believers edifies and blesses us in unexpected ways if we try again.

Despite everyone's best efforts and interventions, Jack loses hope. *Home* details his slide into despair in more vivid detail than *Gilead*. Initially, he seems purposeful and even hopeful. As he cares for his father, works around the house, talks with Glory, fixes the DeSoto, he finds his stride for a little while, seeming optimistic at times. Glory notices the hidden beauty in him, a beauty obscured by a lifetime of inveterate bad habits and poor decisions. For a while he keeps these at bay while he productively participates in family life and hatches a plan to bring Della and Robby to Gilead to start a new life together unmolested by the miscegenation laws and protected by family and friends. But slowly the old problems return—drinking, in particular—and the obstacles to reuniting with his wife and son seem insuperable. Eventually, he succumbs to despair in a botched suicide attempt.

Glory finds him in the barn, slumped against the DeSoto, the car he had invested so much time and energy restoring. Still too drunk to feel the full weight of embarrassment or register Glory's visceral shock, he jokes with her: "Spare a dime, lady? . . . It's your brother Jack. . . . Your brother Jack without his disguise."[47] The night before, drunk and despondent, he gave into despair and tried to end his seemingly hopeless existence. He stuffed his shirt and socks into the tailpipe and tried to hotwire the car into life to end his own, having given the keys over to Glory the night before to prevent an impulsive trip to the town bar. Fortunately, he fails. "I managed to smell like death, at least," he jokes grimly.[48] It seemed somehow fitting: the culmination of a lifetime of failed plans, frustrated aspirations, and self-sabotage. It did not come out of the blue, as we see more clearly in *Jack*. Earlier he confided to Glory his exhaustion with his wayward existence, his inability to find his way to himself.[49]

Characteristically, Glory does her best to salvage the situation, to clean the grime off Jack and to cover for him with their father. She sets him outside in the sun, washes him with soapy water, dries him, and brings him water and a change of clothes. "Ah Jack, she thought. He looked like destitution."[50] Shock and sadness faded to give rise to a new reaction: anger. "He studied her face. 'You're furious.' 'That's right.' 'I can't say I blame you.' 'Don't talk.' He looked away. There was grief in his expression, a kind of bewilderment."[51] He apologizes indirectly: "I'd never have done that if I'd been sober." "It's over now," Glory responds. Jack smiles, a smile of regret, resignation, and realization: "He smiled at her as if to say, No, it isn't, and it won't be."[52] Soon after, as he lay in bed, he nestled into his pillows in a state of reprieve rather than rest, as if to say to himself: "That's all over now, or Now at least I know it will be over sometime."[53]

"He was so tired of himself."[54] What do we do with those who have reached the end of themselves and their futile attempts at joy, peace, and happiness? What do we do if we find ourselves in the cold grip of despair, when we reach rock bottom only to discover it is a ceiling for a deeper abyss that opens beneath us? It is important to normalize experiences of spiritual disorientation in the life of the soul. These periods are common: the dark night of the soul, the state of desolation, feelings of hopelessness. They should not surprise us. They are part of the journey of the soul as it moves through time and traverses its peaks and valleys. Life is not a moveable feast, where we lilt from one cocktail party to another, enjoying the people, places, and high times of life, an endless Gatsby ball. We may enjoy periods of spiritual sunshine and consolation, where the soul shines in seemingly endless ways, but inevitably those times give way to times of darkness.

If you are inside a time like that, hear these three things, spoken in love. First, know that you are not alone. You are not the first person to have been engulfed in darkness and you will not be the last. God inhabits the darkness with you, even when you cannot see or hear Him. He is there. And because He has been through the darkness, He knows it intimately, from the inside. Second, know that you are loved. That is the central tenet of Christianity: you are deeply loved. Even though you might not feel lovable, you are loved. God is love, and God's love engulfs you, and will overcome the darkness. Third, know that the darkness will eventually lift. Pain is not forever. Loneliness is not eternal. The fog will lift, the light will break through. In the meantime, look for points of light, shafts of grace. In the deepest darkness light will come from unexpected places to illuminate your darkness. Keep your eyes on the horizon: joy comes in the morning.[55]

If you are outside a time of darkness, you might remember a time like that in your life. Those in a state of spiritual desolation require an extra measure of grace: patience, attention, and love. In their condition, however, they are often not able to receive grace easily. They may push you away. They may reject you entirely. They will not always hear you and see what you are trying to say and do to and for them. Be patient. Speak simply. Give them basic principles to cling to, like spiritual life-preservers. To know that you are not alone, to know that you are loved, to know that it will not last forever can keep people afloat. Blame, advice, and even theology can weigh them down if done in the wrong way, in the wrong proportions. Just listen. Be there. Do things with them, familiar activities that coax them back to life, that help them to discover or rediscover themselves and the joy of life. Do not set timetables. Do not rush things. Healing takes time.

Most of all, know that you cannot heal them.[56] We cannot fix anyone or any situation. Every person must take responsibility for their own journey, for their own healing, for their own home-finding.[57] We are not promised any outcomes. Jack's mother dies without seeing him restored to her. Glory, with all her love and goodness, with every good intention, cannot fix Jack, cannot allay his self-recrimination, cannot prevent his suicide attempt. She makes him food and coffee and prepares his room, but she cannot make him feel at home in the end. She is not to blame. It was not her burden to bear, only her deepest desire. We can shower someone with *agape* love—self-sacrificial, giving, other-centered love—for an entire lifetime without any guarantees. Old Boughton loves Jack despite all the heartaches, through all the disappointments of waiting and wondering, yet to no avail. In the end, it was up to Jack and Jack alone to forge a way home or to make a new home. Every soul must find its own way in the world, to find its reason, and to inhabit the vaulted ceilings and hidden depths of themselves.

Jack rolls away from Gilead dejected, believing that he has caused undue stress for Glory and his father. He refuses to endure the death of his father and the reunion of a family he has always felt outside of and adjacent to, inexplicably, even to himself.[58] We do not know his destination. As readers we can hope for the best, hope for a new beginning where he can build a life for himself and his family. Perhaps his time at home has helped him, grounding, encouraging, and reorienting him in ways that will facilitate his flourishing. Perhaps another environment will activate him: different people and places shape and reshape the soul in profound ways, after all. Perhaps. Souls wander this world at different paces and in different ways. The journey is harder for some than others. That is part of the mystery of existence. Jack struggles while Teddy thrives and we do not know the reason.

Glory stays in their childhood home as an act of faith and testament to her undying love for Jack.[59] When she finally meets Della and discovers the existence of her nephew Robert, she realizes she could never possibly leave. She would stay, tend to the house Jack secretly loved, safeguard the family memories, harbor hope, and curate *caritas*—love—despite her wounds, perhaps because of them. Thus, her life will become a monument to love and hope: "Maybe this Robert will come back someday. . . . And I will be almost old. . . . He will talk to me a little while, too shy to tell me why he has come, and then he will thank me and leave. . . . He is young. He cannot know that my whole life has come down to this moment."[60] Is she a martyr or a hero? How we answer that evaluative question tells us more about us than her. Glory is a "good soul," as Jack says, and she chooses to bind her soul to his, regardless of the cost.[61] It becomes her "reason to live this life," and it is sufficient.[62]

Conclusion

Wounded souls do not forfeit their beauty. They sometimes hide it from others because they fail to see that the wound itself creates unexpected beauty around it. Wounds can engender tenderness, empathy, wisdom, perspective, kindness, grace, and a plethora of other spiritual qualities. They direct us to other and sometimes new aspects of the self that dazzle in ways that would not have appeared without them. Should we thank God for our wounds? Maybe the most spiritual among us can. Maybe we can at least recognize the ways God uses them to recreate us, to mold us into something new. At the very least we can thank God for the souls who partially patch up our wounds, who make life bearable, who help us endure them and discover the beauty concealed in them. Wounds are sacred. They show us who we are, where we have been. Jesus does not parade his wounds, and yet he shows them when necessary.[63]

Old Boughton, Jack, and Glory, these beautiful, wounded, embattled souls, share a sacred time together, navigating their respective crises and extending as much grace and hospitality to each other as they can. Slowly Jack learns to trust Glory with some of his wounds but never fully, hence the surprise revelation about his son. Glory knows not to trust Jack with her deepest wounds, especially since he has the older brother tendency to poke fun at sensitive subjects, but she trusts him enough to share some of her misadventures in love.[64] In fact, they bond over their wounds—sometimes laughing, sometimes crying—in a spiritual solidarity of brokenness where they protect each other's dignity and privacy with tenderness. In the end, although they do not save or heal each other, they make life more livable. In their gentleness, attentiveness, and kindness, they catch glimpses of the beauty their wounds conceal and reveal. We might not be able to help a soul find its way home, but we can walk with them as they search for it, even when they have lost their way.

Notes

1 Emily Barton, "Slowly but Surely," *Los Angeles Times*, September 7, 2008, https://www.latimes.com/archives/la-xpm-2008-sep-07-ca-marilynne-robinson7-story.html.

2 A. O. Scott, "Return of the Prodigal Son," *New York Times*, September 21, 2008, https://www.nytimes.com/2008/09/21/books/review/Scott-t.html.

3 Engebretson, *Understanding Marilynne Robinson*, 56.

4 Tanner, *The Elusive Everyday in the Fiction of Marilynne Robinson*, 91.

5 Tanner, *The Elusive Everyday in the Fiction of Marilynne Robinson*, 91.

6 I use the term advisedly. In a sense, *Home* is a family "reading" of Jack through the eyes of Glory. Jack serves as its underlying, enigmatic, sacred "text": "the real text was Jack." Marilynne Robinson, *Home* (New York: Farrar, Straus & Giroux, 2008), 45. The Gilead saga offers different "readings" of Jack, including Ames's hermeneutic of suspicion that ultimately transforms into a hermeneutic of grace, Old Boughton's hermeneutic of grace that finally devolves into a hermeneutic of exhaustion, Della's hermeneutic of generosity and hope, her father's hermeneutic of hostility, etc. Jack not only represents a theological question about the relationship between predestination and free will. He also represents a philosophical question about identity: Who is the real Jack? Which hermeneutic most accurately captures his essence, or do all viewpoints ultimately distort as much as they reveal? Who can best depict a life, interpret the various strands that interweave into our complex selves? Ultimately, I think the Gilead saga leaves these questions open, opting instead to show how Jack means different things to different people, refusing to render any final judgments.

7 For instance, the conversation about predestination contains many significant similarities and differences. Robinson, *Gilead*, 149–53; *Home*, 219–28.

8 Robinson, *Home*, 31, 115, 158.

9 Robinson, *Home*, 3. These opening words have a foreshadowing effect: "And, depending on how you read [it], the opening of the novel 'Home to stay, Glory!' announced the end of Glory's part of the story before it begins too." Tiffany Eberle Kriner, "Space/

Time/Doctrine: Marilynne Robinson's Gilead Novels," in Larsen and Johnson, ed., *Balm in Gilead*, 132.

10 Robinson, *Home*, 3.

11 Robinson, *Home*, 149.

12 Robinson, *Home*, 118–19. "It was a long engagement. A policeman saw me and came over to ask me what I was doing. I told him I was throwing away four hundred fifty-two love letters and one cheap ring. . . . It was all horrible enough to be funny, I suppose." Robinson, *Home*, 119.

13 Robinson, *Home*, 136–37.

14 Robinson, *Home*, 150, 233, 276–77; cf. *Gilead*, 156–60.

15 Robinson, *Home*, 258.

16 Robinson, *Home*, 30.

17 Robinson, *Home*, 208; cf. *Gilead*, 217ff.

18 Robinson, *Home*, 274, 295.

19 Robinson, *Home*, 317.

20 Robinson, *Home*, 102.

21 Robinson, *Home*, 97–98, 135, 235–36.

22 "But you were always off somewhere." Robinson, *Home*, 175. Jack's sense of estrangement mixes with love: "I've thought about this place so many times. When I was a kid I used to wish I lived here. I used to wish I could just walk in the door like the rest of you did and, you know, sit down at the table and do my homework or something. . . . I was usually closer to home than he thought I was." Robinson, *Home*, 276.

23 Robinson, *Home*, 172. "He was so tired of himself." Robinson, *Home*, 257.

24 Robinson, *Home*, 282.

25 Robinson, *Home*, 31–32, 41.

26 "Kindness takes more strength than I have now." Robinson, *Home*, 274.

27 Robinson, *Home*, 206–7.

28 Robinson, *Gilead*, 230–31.

29 Robinson, *Gilead*, 128.

30 Robinson, *Gilead*, 123.

31 Robinson, *Gilead*, 128.

32 Robinson, *Gilead*, 128–29.

33 Robinson, *Gilead*, 131.

34 Robinson, *Gilead*, 131.

35 Robinson, *Gilead*, 141.
36 Robinson, *Gilead*, 144; *Home*, 216.
37 Robinson, *Home*, 212.
38 Robinson, *Home*, 206.
39 Robinson, *Home*, 207.
40 Robinson, *Home*, 207.
41 Robinson, *Home*, 211.
42 Robinson, *Home*, 212.
43 Robinson, *Home*, 212.
44 Robinson, *Home*, 213–14.
45 Robinson, *Home*, 207.
46 "You have to forgive me for that. That was such a foolish thing to say. I'm tired. I'm old." Robinson, *Gilead*, 231.
47 Robinson, *Home*, 243.
48 Robinson, *Home*, 245.
49 Robinson, *Home*, 172; cf. 257.
50 Robinson, *Home*, 249.
51 Robinson, *Home*, 250.
52 Robinson, *Home*, 250.
53 Robinson, *Home*, 251.
54 Robinson, *Home*, 257.
55 Psalm 30:5.
56 "That old illusion that she could help her father with the grief Jack caused, the grief Jack was, when it was as far beyond her power to soothe or mitigate as the betrayal of Judas Iscariot." Robinson, *Home*, 248.
57 "The poor old devil feels responsible for my soul." Robinson, *Home*, 143.
58 Robinson, *Home*, 259, 269.
59 Jack often betrays his secret love of the family home, especially the barn, his abode of solitude, where he embodies both his desire to be a part of the family and his feeling of being outside of it. As he prepares to leave, he looks around the house wistfully, and Glory realizes both his complex bond with it and the enormous impact it has on her. "She thought, Dear Lord, he is missing it all in anticipation. She thought, As long as he is alive in the world, or as long as no one knows otherwise, I will probably have to keep all that sour, fierce, dreary black walnut. That purple rug. And if he dies I will

still have to keep it, because I have seen him look at it in this way." Robinson, *Home*, 299.

60 Robinson, *Home*, 324–25.

61 Robinson, *Home*, 118, 149.

62 "There are a thousand thousand reasons to live this life, every one of them sufficient." Robinson, *Gilead*, 243.

63 John 20:27.

64 Robinson, *Home*, 119, 149.

6

Embattled Souls in *Lila* and *Jack*

Lila

> When you're scalded, touch hurts, it makes
> no difference if it's kindly meant.
>
> —Marilynne Robinson, *Lila*

The Gilead universe expands in *Lila* (2014) and *Jack* (2020).[1] These eponymous novels delineate the hitherto murky background of their title characters.[2] They belong to the Gilead world despite their setting primarily outside of it. Lila and Jack's convoluted histories, hinted at in *Gilead* (2004) and *Home* (2008), are disclosed. As they narrate their thoughts and experiences, their multifaceted personalities come into sharper focus, explaining puzzling behaviors in the first two novels. While the third and fourth volumes of the series do not have the spiritual force of the first two, they nonetheless develop the story of two precious souls foundational to the fictional landscape Robinson crafts, clarifying the complex dynamics at play. Or, to stay with Robinson's musical analogy, they extend the melodies sounded in *Gilead* and *Home*, creating a fuller symphony of soul. Consequently, *Lila* and *Jack* are best seen as supplemental to *Gilead* and *Home*.

To characterize them as supplemental diminishes neither their autonomy nor their contribution to the series. Both have moments of aching beauty, and both illuminate aspects of the characters that were left opaque in the first two. Moreover, to treat them together does not devalue as much as it contextualizes: as the third and fourth books of the cycle, they build off the foundations of the first two, so we need not come to the title characters as if for the first time in an artificial gesture of respect. We already know these characters: their distinctive notes and motifs are not new to Robinson's readers. Or at least we *think* we know them. As we read, we discover that they are much more multifaceted than we realized, which provides fresh opportunities for analysis of how they raise spiritual problematics and expand questions begun in the first two novels.

In different ways, *Lila* and *Jack* illustrate the endless interplay between solitude and companionship. On the one hand, the soul is always alone with itself, privy to its hidden hopes and dreams, desires and wounds. On the other hand, it reaches out of its inner precincts for companionship. This dynamic interpersonal interchange surfaces several significant spiritual questions, including the host of difficulties involved in bridging the gap between souls, especially embattled souls, who bear many scars, often unseen. When souls are beset by problems and pain, they often retreat inward and lash out against those seeking to help them. We see that with Lila and Ames and with Jack and Ames throughout the series. As we explore the intricacies of navigating soul solitude and soul companionship in these novels, we will focus on the barriers to intimacy, the dangers of uniting with other souls, and the beauty of relationships forged out of the fires of tribulations.

Lila, told in the disjointed, deeply interior voice of its heroine, reaches back to the hazy memories of Lila's childhood. Several times in *Gilead* Ames intimates to their son that her life had been very hard.[3] In *Lila* we see just how hard it had been, more than he knew.[4] As an infant she was abandoned by her parents to a shady boarding house, only to be neglected before Doll abducts her: "If I left her where she was, she'da died for sure."[5] They take to the open road with itinerate field hands, working for day wages, perpetually at risk. Eventually the work dries up, so she leaves that life for work in a brothel. After that time plays out, she works in a hotel for a while and then wanders until she finds herself in Gilead, a strange town with a "big, silvery old" minister who notices her and eventually falls in love with her.[6] As she settles uneasily into her new life, she never feels at home, ponders the storms of existence, and itches to return to the open road.[7]

Spiritually, as a first principle, Lila teaches us that everyone comes from somewhere, that everyone has a backstory, and that everyone fights internal battles that began long ago. For Ames, as for most in Gilead, Lila remains a mystery. She conceals more than she reveals, leaving it to Ames's imagination to fill in the gaps. He knows she has had a hard life, although he does not know most of the details. The mystery of her past leads to several complications and confusions. The complications range from misreading her reticence to misusing her knife—which has profound symbolic meaning for her—for mundane tasks.[8] The confusions include her strange disappearances from town.[9] Ames knows that she does not feel entirely comfortable in their house, in their town, and maybe not even in their marriage, but he tries to make them all as hospitable as possible for her.[10] Lila is an open question, a culmination of tragedies and tribulations he barely knows.[11]

Lila illustrates the irreducible mystery of souls. Truly knowing another person takes tremendous effort and insight, and we never exhaust their hidden depths. Everyone's past informs the present. Their experiences, positive and negative, inflect their behavior in ways that are not always immediately evident. People naturally present a socially acceptable version of themselves that we too often take as given, as sufficient to understand who they are and how we should engage with them. To facilitate interpersonal interactions, we instinctively fit people into familiar categories and paradigms without fully appreciating the mystery of their otherness. When we over-interpret their self-presentation and see them through a typological lens we miss the mystery of their existence, the surplus they do not show and that we cannot see. Ironically, Ames knows Lila intimately as his wife and twilight companion and simultaneously does not really know her at all.

This knowing-yet-not-knowing duality creates daily tensions and dysfunctions in relationships. A spouse takes offense at an ostensibly inoffensive comment, a friend overreacts to a seemingly benign action, a boss erupts over trivial matters, a stranger becomes apoplectic over a minor traffic provocation. Conflict and confusion bewilder us because we forget the mystery of their otherness, encapsulated in the adage: "Everyone's fighting a battle you don't know about." The truth is deeper than the bumper sticker. Everyone is existing in ways we do not know about, reacting in ways that reflect past traumas and conditioning, and interacting with others in ways they only partly apprehend because they do not fully grasp their own hidden depths. We also inhabit and operate in the world in ways that we do not fully comprehend for the very same reasons. Connecting our deep, damaged, disparate souls requires delicate bridge building.

Building bridges takes time, care, and patience. It begins with small exchanges and then expands. If we rush the process, we will overlook vital pieces of the puzzle of the soul. Eventually this will lead to misunderstanding and miscommunication. For instance, Lila feels antipathy toward Ames's best friend: "Lila hated Boughton."[12] She feels self-conscious about her grammar and education, which Boughton aggravates by his inadvertent condescension. As a slightly pedantic pastor, Old Boughton naturally identifies and corrects verbal mistakes: "I believe Boughton made her self-conscious with that little trick of his of correcting people. Not that he ever corrected her."[13] It is just a habit, a bad habit he seems unaware of. If Lila had recognized and dismissed it as the byproduct of years of reading and preaching, and if Old Boughton had considered her sensitivity, they might have been able to establish a connection, even a friendship.

Soul growth requires constant adaptation in the face of change. New people and places force us to adapt, often to the point of reshaping. Lila wrestles with adapting to Gilead and her new role as a pastor's wife. In some ways she resists it, sometimes to the point of abandoning the project altogether. In other ways she embraces it: reading scripture, adopting new social conventions, teaching her boy hymns. Similarly, Ames must adapt to having a new wife who is very different from his first wife, to learn her ways of being and to adjust to her personality. These adaptations and adjustments require knowledge of the other and willingness to incorporate their distinctive sensibilities and sensitivities into our actions without—crucially—losing our soul-shape. The tension between retaining the self while making room for others lies at the heart of interpersonal relationships. To what extent have we expanded our souls to make room for others? Are we willing to trade solitude for companionship, and in what proportions?

Spiritually, Lila also illustrates the emotional and interpersonal challenges of trauma. Lila is a deeply traumatized person. Abandonment, abduction, abuse, exploitation, and violence scar her soul, impacting her ability to trust. In *The Elusive Everyday in the Fiction of Marilynne Robinson*, Laura Tanner lists the various ways Lila reiterates her distrust in the novel: "I just can't trust you at all" (58); "I don't trust nobody," "Can't trust nobody" (69, 78); "Nobody to trust" (82); "I don't trust nobody" (89); "I can't trust you" (89; cf. 95, 116).[14] Her distrust, based on her past trauma, makes perfect sense in the context of her life story. How could she trust anyone when those closest to her failed to protect and provide for her? For all she knows, Ames is just another in a long line of caretakers or employers to neglect or take advantage of her. When we have been betrayed and abused by those closest to us, those tasked to care for us, how do we regain trust in others?

Ames uses his pastoral instincts and innate benevolence to take a kind, gentle approach.[15] He gives her space and time. He does not rush or coerce her in any way. Instead, he demonstrates constancy and care: "'Well,' he said. He patted her back. She said, 'I guess I'm tired.' 'Yes, well—' and he put his arms around her, very carefully, very gently."[16] For a woman accustomed to the harsh conditions of reality, Ames's tenderness would seem very foreign, even suspicious. Men in her past were grasping and harsh, but Ames is giving and gentle. She must have wondered: "What is his angle? What game is he playing?" Sometimes she retreats from him, hiding in the fields or in a room. At other times she accosts him with unprovoked meanness. Her retreats and attacks play out past wounds and trauma, even though Ames does not treat her poorly. "When you're scalded, touch hurts, it makes no difference if it's kindly meant."[17]

Imagine the soul, especially its emotive aspect, as a delicate flower. In the dark, cold, and rain, it closes in on itself as a protective mechanism. In the warmth of the sun, however, it opens to its salubrious rays, gaining nourishment for growth. Experience teaches that hurt people will close off from others, turn inward, test others, lash out, act up, and engage in self-sabotaging behavior. Ames might not have understood the precise details of Lila's trauma, but he knew enough to know a hurt soul when he saw one. He also knew woundedness himself, albeit of a different sort. Day by day, she learns to trust him more, tries to be kind, and grows to appreciate him. But it takes time. "Did I ever say that? That I love you?" Lila asks.[18] It is not an easy thing for her to say. All she knew of love before Ames were distorted versions, laced with self-interest, often driven by desperation. With Ames she starts to bloom. Warm souls like Ames help us to unclench, open, and flourish. If you are thinking of someone who does that for you, let them know it.

Questions remain, however. Why did she have to endure so much suffering? Why did she find herself in no-win situations, where the cards seemed constantly stacked against her? The warm embrace of Ames cannot stop the cold winds of widowhood that await her, and they both know it:

"I'll be leaving you on your own. We've both always known that. I can't tell you how deeply I regret it."[19] Lila knows her way around hard times. She wonders, however, why they had to be so rock hard and sharp-edged.[20] Significantly, that was her opening cosmological query to him when they first met: "I just been wondering lately why things happen the way they do."[21] Ames understands that question well: "I've been wondering about that more or less my whole life."[22] Years of preaching and reading and suffering did not yield a ready answer for him: "You asked me why things happen the way they do, and I had to say I didn't know. I still don't. But the question is interesting."[23]

Interesting indeed, and persistent for Lila, given her traumatic life experiences. It does not take a theologian or philosopher to question why God permits suffering. Anyone reflecting on the ways of the world can pose it clearly and authentically. Lila poses it to Ames in the form of the suffering of a baby: "'But I did mean to ask you sometime,' she said. 'There's a baby cast out in a field, just thrown away. And it's God that picks her up. But why would God let somebody throw her out like that in the first place?'"[24] Lila must have felt like that abandoned baby more than once in her life: cast aside, discarded, and unattended. "But if God really has all that power, why does He let children get treated so bad? Because they are sometimes. That's true."[25] Her life illustrates the problem of evil: Why would a God of unlimited power and unbounded goodness allow all the evil that befalls her? For Lila, the autobiographical, the story of her difficult life, raises the abiding theoretical question.

For suffering souls, the question intensifies when directed inward. Why me? Why did God allow it to happen? Why is life so hard? What did I do to deserve such misfortune? Sometimes those who suffer feel cosmically targeted, as if the universe is conspiring against them. For Lila, the question touches on the central fact of her existence: continual hardship and suffering. Where is God in all that? How does she live and think through life day by day given the indignities and indigence of her past? Ames allays her angst not as a preacher or theologian, but as a fellow sufferer. Ames helps because he knows suffering from the inside, like her, regardless of the type of suffering in question. Lila instinctively recognizes his experiential solidarity with her. He might not be able to answer the question to her theological satisfaction, but he honestly affirms and addresses it, and ultimately responds to it by inhabiting suffering with her.

The spiritual life forces us to reckon with suffering, to come to terms with it for ourselves and others. In fact, navigating suffering is one of the primary purposes of religion. Theologians confront suffering at a theoretical level when they formulate the problem of evil and entertain various theodicies, that is, rational explanations of why a good and all-powerful God would permit evil. For Lila and Ames, however, it is not primarily an abstract question in search of a sound theological or philosophical answer. No, for them it is a personal cry in search of a hearer, or Hearer. Who will hear their hurt and heartache, their anger and angst? As they share their pain and confess their confusion, they begin to find comfort and healing. The intellectual question—Where is God in all this hurt?—is secondary to the existential question: Who will walk with me through all this hurt? Who will grieve with me, cry with me, and hope with me?

Like Lila, we must ask these difficult questions about the meaning of our suffering. Sidestepping them only forestalls its acceptance and integration, thereby preventing growth. Bottling them inside risks later destructive eruptions, often in unrelated areas, as the pressure builds from the unresolved emotions. Surfacing painful memories obviously comes with risks, however. It can plunge us back into dark times emotionally, which might make matters worse. Sharing with a friend, pastor, priest, counselor, therapist, and other wise and empathetic souls might help us navigate these fraught questions and mitigate their potentially explosive emotional reverberations. It takes a brave soul to tackle painful memories and honestly ask the questions they raise without any guarantee of a comforting answer. No wonder so many simply ignore them, relegating them to the background: fear, uncertainty, and isolation immobilize us if we surrender to them.

Like Ames, we need not have the answers, either for ourselves or others. Often we want to alleviate the pain of others through answers to their pressing questions. False certitudes might satisfy momentarily, but in the long run their speciousness will be exposed. Better to admit ignorance, or partial knowledge, and gently listen, affirm, and guide to the extent that we are asked for guidance. Often, however, people just need to feel heard, to have the opportunity to express inner turmoil to a safe person, rather than receive advice or answers. If Ames had responded to Lila's question with an analysis of the cosmic implications of free will for human existence, he would have pushed her away. She was not really looking for a theodicy. She was looking for companionship in suffering. Answers have a way of dismissing the question *and* the questioner. They close conversation rather than open it to deeper dialogue that creates a sense of solidarity in suffering.

But beyond her suffering, who is Lila? Her parents did not even bother to name her.[26] "Lila" was the name of the sister of an old woman who helped them early in their flight from the boarding house.[27] More than most, Lila's name reflects her shifting social contexts, not her inner self. Over the course of her life her name changes from Baby to Lila to Lila Dahl to Rosie to Lila Ames.[28] At one level, her names are arbitrary, more social codes than soul designations. At another level, they reveal the circumstantial transitions she undergoes. As we move to different places, interact with different people, assume different roles, our names might alter. Given names, nicknames, titles, functions, all swirl together to signify us, our souls. No name, however, captures the totality of the soul: no title exhausts it, no role encompasses it. Yet, society requires stable identification to function, so we have our official names, but our souls are much more profound, dynamic, ineffable, and multifaceted.

Spiritually, names signify both the ways our contexts shape us and the mystery of the self. Lila receives her names based on the situations she finds herself in, most not of her own volition. In that sense they are arbitrary and sometimes false, like Rosie. Lila was Rosie for a time in St. Louis when she worked in a brothel, mostly doing menial housework.[29] Pseudonymity was the standard practice, a way of protecting their identity and creating an emotional distance from the work.[30] Names help us remember our past, our commitments, and our roles, but they can also shackle us if they limit the full expression of the soul. If we are only the bearers of our family history, or our chosen profession, or our chosen roles, then the unseen depths of the soul might never rise to the surface. We need not discard these names, but we ought to recognize the surplus of the soul beyond them. The notion of receiving a new name in heaven (Revelation 2:17) hints at our hidden depths.

Names, then, signify beyond themselves, embedding histories in their designations. Similarly, objects have meanings beyond their intrinsic function and worth. Doll's shawl and knife have strong symbolic import for Lila. Doll's shawl signifies the warmth and cover of a caregiver.[31] It has maternal connotations for Lila, despite the fact that Doll was not her mother. Thus, when Doane set the shawl ablaze as retaliation for Doll's rebuke for leaving Lila on the church steps, they lost far more than a tattered rag.[32] Still, Lila preserves it in her memory. Memory redeems it from the flames. Doll's knife signifies provision and protection. It has paternal connotations, despite the fact that Doll was not her father. Ironically, Doll uses the knife—maybe against Lila's own father—for protection.[33] So when Ames uses the knife for mundane purposes, it desacralizes it.[34] Lila decides to keep the knife, after much deliberation and reflection on its violent past.[35] It is her way of remembering and redeeming the past.

Think of the objects that have deep symbolic value for you, the keepsakes that you have treasured through the years. Most likely, they were gifts from family or friends, or tokens of affection, or markers of victories and accomplishments. These types of physical objects serve to remind us of formative people, places, and events. In other words, they testify to our presence in the world, the distinctive stamp we leave. In a way, they are sacred relics, not in the conventional religious sense, but relics of our soul. Like the shawl and knife for Lila, we affix meaning and strong emotional associations to items that symbolize pivotal moments or people. Beyond their intrinsic value, they are monuments to love, given and received. They anchor us to the world, reminding us of who we are, where we have been, and who we have journeyed with. They cannot be bought or sold or appraised because they are part of a different economy, the economy of the soul.

Soul relics—the objects we imbue with sacred significance—call for special care.[36] Sometimes we put them in prominent places in our home where they testify to major moments, connections, or accomplishments, such us as family pictures, special gifts, and diplomas. Sometimes we put them in hidden places, our wallet, purse, or bedroom, as private reminders, such as a small picture or note or keepsake. Where we display them depends on the object and its signification. As we move through the day, the months, the years, as we move locations and vocations, as we move through time itself, gaining and losing family and friends, they mark our passage and serve as threads of continuity sewn through the disparate cords of our lives. They preserve family histories, incarnate memories, embody stories, and mark accomplishments, keeping us tethered to ourselves through the ebbs and flow of time and space. They ground us.

Above all, however, people shape souls. Lila's soul is intertwined with others, especially Doll's: "She lived for Doll to see."[37] Doll dominates her consciousness. In fact, she is Lila's alter-ego, an internal sounding board for her lonely thoughts and a litmus test for her values. Doll's soul, however spiritually endangered according to traditional theological accounts, shapes Lila's, so she remains loyal to her even in her imagination, even if it means perdition ultimately: "If Doll was going to be lost forever, Lila wanted to be right there with her, holding to the skirt of her dress."[38] She returns to that thought near the end of the novel: "And then she thought, I couldn't bear to be without Doll, or Mellie, or Doane and Marcelle. Even Arthur and his boys . . ." because her soul was stamped with the sense of fairness they instilled: "If there was goodness at that center of things, that one rule would have to be respected, because it was as important to them as anything in this world."[39]

Souls shape us in ways that vary from person to person, and even differ with a single person. Doane and his group of field hands sometimes treat Lila kindly and at other times cruelly. Doll shapes Lila in positive and negative ways. And yet, despite the mixed impact of her companions, they are as internal to her as her own solitary consciousness. In fact, they are so fused to her soul that she cannot imagine life—here or beyond—without them. Similarly, the souls that have shaped us stay with us, even though some have hurt us. To the extent that we have traveled through life with them, they belong with us. If they have done us harm, we must learn to forgive them, to see them through the lens of grace, and to let go of the bitterness that will devour us from within if we hold on to it. If they have blessed us, enriched our souls, we should be grateful for their legacy of love and seek to expand it. Love always gives.

Love is seeing the beauty in another soul. Lila repeatedly notes Ames's beauty to herself. "And he was beautiful for an old man."[40] "He was a beautiful old man."[41] "He is such a beautiful old man."[42] Given the weight of her existence, with all its shame and suffering, she finds herself unwilling or unable to receive his love fully, to trust in it: "I can't love you as much as I love you. I can't feel as happy as I am."[43] As they ponder the complexity of their love, she realizes she may have never expressed it to him properly before: "I'm going to make us some more coffee. Did I ever say that? That I love you? I always thought it sounded a little foolish. But the way you talk, sometime I might regret putting it off."[44] In the end, she receives his love as fully as she can, within the confines of her emotional limitations, her guardedness. And she loves him as he is, despite being "so damn old,"[45] even though he never really did answer her question.[46]

Lila and Ames retain their solitude despite their solidarity. They share the complexities of suffering, including missing some aspects of their old lives, despite it. "'I got so much life behind me.' 'I know.' 'It was nothing like this life.' 'I know.' 'I miss it sometimes.' He nodded. 'We aren't so different. There are things I miss.'"[47] Here their solitudes converge around a shared sense of suffering, not the other's particular suffering, but the experience of suffering itself. There are things they can share and things they cannot: secret joys, hidden hopes, ineffable truths, unspeakable heartaches. They share what they can, always treasuring a hidden surplus. *Lila* ends on a hopeful note, gesturing toward a deeper communion between their solitudes: "Someday she would tell him what she knew."[48] Not today. Maybe not tomorrow. But on some hopeful day she will dip from the wells of herself to refresh Ames's soul with more of *her*.

Jack

> I just think there has to be a Jesus, to say "beautiful" about things no one else would see.
>
> —Marilynne Robinson, *Jack*

With *Jack*, we reach the end of the fictional universe of Gilead, and of our spiritual meditations. In *Gilead*, Jack bursts onto the scene as a disruption to Ames's twilight ruminations.[49] At first we see a captious depiction of Jack, filtered through the suspicious lens of a not-yet-fully-sanctified Ames, who obsesses over Jack's misdeeds, character flaws, and potential dangers to his family. Later, after Jack shares with him his secret love and burden, Ames begins to see him through the eyes of grace.[50] In *Home*, we see Jack under a different light, from Glory's loving and protective perspective.[51] She sees his goodness, talent, beauty, and fragility. Glory never deviates in her love and loyalty to her wayward brother, his second abandonment of her notwithstanding.[52] Jack illustrates the complexity of souls and the plurality of ways to understand them. For some, Jack's soul dazzles and delights; for others, it infuriates and inflames. Sometimes it does both to the same person.

With Jack, there is always more than meets the eye. His dress and mannerisms suggest a gentleman, but he often acts like a scoundrel. His drinking and lying suggest degeneracy, but he often behaves with dignity.[53] "You're just trouble," Della says to him prophetically, exasperated. "He nodded. 'I've never denied it. Seldom denied it, anyway.'"[54] Despite the danger, Della finds herself falling in love with him. She sees beyond the trouble to his talent, beyond the brokenness to his beauty, both vividly illustrated in his love of poetry. Even the mock poetry he inscribes in her returned copy of *Hamlet* has hidden gems: "Had I a blessing, even one, / Its grace would light on you alone. / Had I a single living prayer / It would attend you, mild as air. / Had my heart an unbroken string / ring sing sting cling thing / Oh, I am ill at these numbers! / IOU a dollar. And a book. / Long Farewell!"[55] Della sees the depth he conceals and abuses with drink, dark humor, and aimlessness.

Jack internalizes his sense of damnation. "I am the Prince of Darkness," he says and thinks to himself repeatedly.[56] Repeat a negative thought to yourself enough times and you become it. It becomes a psychological self-fulfilling prophecy. Without sliding into the speciousness of prosperity gospel, or spiritualizing the current enthusiasm for "manifesting" success, it is worth noting the power of internal narratives. We often enact the interior stories we tell ourselves about ourselves. If Jack is the Prince of Darkness, as he claims, then his destiny is destruction, which he believes. He then plays out the script he has written for himself through destructive behavior, which reinforces his internal narrative, creating a vicious cycle.[57] Jack spirals downward in life because he isolates himself from the love of those around him who would disrupt his supposed predestined damnation, who would offer him a different story to inhabit.

His self-delusion operates at multiple levels. No, Jack is not the embodiment of evil, not destined to the misery he continually inflicts on himself and others as he externalizes his fatalistic internal narrative.[58] Nor, however, does he truly strive for an unobtrusive, innocuous existence, as he supposes: "I aspire to utter harmlessness. It's a contest I have with myself. I have no real aptitude for harmlessness, which makes it interesting."[59] Jack continually tells himself that he simply wants a harmless life, but, bafflingly to him, seems unable to realize that goal.[60] In his mind, it is as if catastrophe unfairly and inexplicably befalls him without his involvement as a cosmic manifestation and confirmation of his predetermined damnation. But that is a lie. Jack leaves a trail of human carnage in his wake not by destiny, but by deliberate misconduct. Often he knows his actions are wrong and destructive and does it anyway, with an air of innocent bewilderment when negative consequences ensue.

Two types of self-delusions immobilize Jack, precluding his rehabilitation: spiritual fatalism and moral evasion. The first prevents his embrace of grace. The second prevents him from taking responsibility for his misdeeds. Most self-delusions contain some truth, usually a secondary truth that obscures a primary truth, as we have seen. Yes, Jack struggles to stay on the straight and narrow, but that does not mean he is predestined to hell. Yes, Jack does not often intentionally and directly try to hurt others, but his selfishness and incorrigibility predictably lead to harm. At some level, maybe subconsciously, he is *trying* to hurt others. Perhaps that is just another way he externalizes his pernicious sense of reprobation. Perhaps it is just a reflection of his character, which has been marred by a lifetime of working against his own happiness and therefore the happiness of those he interacts with, especially those who love him most.

Della creates a whole new narrative for Jack to internalize. With her he transforms from a bum, thief, and drunk to a gallant gentleman, beginning with their first interaction when he helps her to collect her scattered papers in the rain.[61] She loves him, despite his conspicuous flaws. She sees his inner beauty: his love of poetry and literature, his sensitivity and manners. They have long, lovely, literary conversations, memorably in the Bellefontaine cemetery.[62] For the first time in a long time, maybe in his life, he feels *seen*. Della's gift to Jack is to see his soul, as she tries to explain to him: "But once in a lifetime, maybe, you look at a stranger and you see a soul, a glorious presence out of place in the world. And if you love God, every choice is made for you. There is no turning away. You've seen the mystery—you've seen what life is about. What it's for."[63] Of all the beautiful souls she has seen—witnessed—Jack's is "the brightest."[64]

Della has the special gift of spiritual perception, seeing the hidden beauty concealed in troubled souls. It enables her to see beyond the false fronts that Jack creates, but it also exposes her to the danger that faces all who share that gift: susceptibility to harm. Jack warns her many times: "All I mean is that I'm trouble. I might do you real harm, never meaning to." Della responds knowingly: "I bring problems on myself. Some of them are worth it."[65] She overestimates his goodness and underestimates the damage he could do, while he becomes the best version of himself around her. Troubled souls are drawn to pure souls like Della for the light they shine, for their ability to elicit their best, but it comes at a cost. By her own admission, Della is no saint, but contact with Jack, with his self-destructive tendencies, destabilizes her life. She loses her job, sullies her reputation, gets pregnant, and is disowned by her religious family.[66] Ostensibly, meeting Jack destroys her life. She does not, however, see it that way, hence the mystery of love, which can simultaneously destroy and save.

Spiritual perspicacity enables us to see beauty and goodness in souls that others dismiss as irredeemable, as hopeless, as lost. It derives from the recognition of the inherent beauty and dignity of every soul, which only awaits discovery. Cultivating that gift makes life a wonderful adventure where we encounter beauty around every corner and appreciate the distinctive ways each person brings beauty into the world. It is a gift, but it is a gift that contains two hidden dangers. First, projection. Those with finely tuned souls, who have diligently worked on their spiritual life, will often unconsciously project their goodness onto undeserving souls. That is grace, but it backfires if the gift is given *as if* it is deserved, if more credit is given to the recipient than is due, creating the illusion of merit. Second, spiritual contagion. Contact with troubled souls has a contaminating effect after prolonged or intensive exposure. It will cost the giver, and that too is grace. It is a costly grace.

I am not, however, positing a dualistic universe of good and bad souls. Obviously all souls exist on a spiritual continuum where all have fallen and require the interventions of grace. We all travel down the same spiritual "Roman's road" toward grace, with hat in hand. I am not proposing spiritual dualism or elitism. I am arguing, perhaps controversially, that more advanced, mature, peaceful souls will pay a price for entanglement with underdeveloped, immature, troubled souls. The solution is not for pristine souls to withdraw from the world, sealing themselves off in elite spiritual communes, apart from the sooted souls of the world. Christ taught an incarnational, entangling, suffering love: a love that counts the cost, that gets involved in the messiness of the spiritual life. The solution is to recognize the dangers, to renew ourselves in nourishing communities and spiritual practices, and to know when a relationship costs more than we can give.

Della, in other words, knows what she is getting into with Jack. She goes in with eyes wide open. Her roommate warns her, her family threatens her, everyone tries to steer her clear of the slow-moving trainwreck that is Jack.[67] But love does not heed calls to caution. The young know what the old sometimes forget: love does not calculate based on the path of least resistance or the probabilities of success. It plunges in, regardless of the dangers, despite its slim chances. It is a force that goes against our best interests sometimes, including self-preservation. It is that strong. "He was in love with her."[68] Her kindness draws him out of his self-imposed solitary confinement.[69] His gentleness convinces her to take the risk. The odds, however, were decisively stacked against them: "There were a thousand barriers between black Della and his indigent, disreputable self, and mere kindness could not lower any of them so much as an inch."[70]

But he cannot help himself.[71] Della's existence enthralls him. Her voice soothes him: "Wonderful. The sound of her voice was more than a relief to him, quintessentially companionable, as if the two of them were together in the world, uniquely, like two strayed angels, despite anything and everything."[72] Their forbidden love blossoms against all odds: "I fell in love with you in a cemetery," she confesses to Jack, to which he responds: "Is that true? I fell in love with you when you asked me in for tea."[73] Two solitudes, flickering in the night, begin to burn together, giving each other comfort and warmth. Although they face the fierce headwinds of familial and societal disapproval, they cling to each other against the greater foe of existence without each other. They would forever cling together, even apart: soulmates.[74]

It would not be an easy life, as they anticipated. Companionship does not eliminate the shape of the soul. Even after their "marriage" and pregnancy, her family disapproved of him, for good reasons. Even though he loves her deeply, has joined his soul to hers, he cannot escape his propensity for self-sabotage. He still struggles with thoughts of suicide, struggles to keep his temper, struggles to keep a job. Mostly, he struggles to stay sober. Their relationship sentences them to a life of suffering, and they know it: "'What a mess we're in, causing each other all this misery.' 'And this is just the beginning.' 'Promise.' 'Promise.'"[75] These informal vows foreshadow the future of their doomed union, which creates joy and peace and companionship, but also insuperable problems that their love cannot solve, only endure. And so they face constant crises and hardships because love chooses life together with suffering rather than an easy life without the beloved.

Amid Jack's continual inner turmoil magical moments nevertheless occur, some with spiritual significance. Through a strange misunderstanding he finds himself in Mount Zion

Baptist Church, a black church, then at lunch afterwards in the basement, then playing hymns on the piano.[76] Through their hospitality, Jack has moments of transparency. "You're a son of the church, I take it," Pastor Samuel Hutchins gently inquires.[77] "Yes. Not really. My father is a minister. Was. He's still alive. The last I heard. He lost his church. My fault, I believe."[78] Rarely does Jack speak so candidly, and he continues to talk without guile with Pastor Hutchins, who perhaps reminds him of his father: "I'm not at all like him. I look like him. People used to say that. But I know age has been hard on him. Then my mother died."[79] With practiced patience and tact Pastor Hutchins coaxes Jack out of his self-created purgatory to share some of his turmoil.

Hospitality creates the environment where hardened and troubled souls can soften and open. In a short span they welcome Jack warmly, bring him food, give him space, and preserve his dignity. That lays a foundation of trust upon which they can build goodwill, encouragement, and advice. Pastor Hutchins readily perceives Jack's uneasiness and spiritual complexity. He also quickly diagnoses his many problems (self-loathing, alienation, hopelessness, sin, disbelief) and offers remedies (grace, acceptance, hope, repentance, faith). Jack feels comfortable disclosing his atheism and discussing it with him.[80] Spiritually, hospitality makes room for grace and earns us the opportunity to talk about the questions and problems that plague people. Arguments for God's existence rarely transform people spiritually; hospitality and acts of kindness, given without any strings attached, loosen the soil of hardened hearts and water the soil of arid souls. Jack, the self-professed atheist and prodigal son, intuitively turns to ministers to unburden his soul. His spiritual condition clearly has complex layers that require careful excavation, something Ames was not able to do until the end of *Gilead* and Pastor Hutchins was only able to begin in *Jack*.

Jack illustrates a critical and difficult truth: you cannot save the people you love. Della's love cannot save him from his past or his self-destructive tendencies. Glory's love cannot keep him on the straight and narrow, cannot help him feel at home, cannot prevent his suicide attempt. His mother and father's love could not keep him tied to the family, sheltered in its warm embrace, away from the people and places that would do him harm. His brother Teddy could not rescue him from his self-imposed exile any more than he could do his college degree for him, despite his best efforts.[81] Ames's love cannot calm his unsettled soul, cannot answer the theological questions that trouble him. Even his son's love cannot prevent his departure from his life. Jack is surrounded by love—deep, passionate, enduring love—and none of it can save him from himself. It is not the failure of love. It is the reality of agency: every soul must find its own way home or wander in the dark.

This is a difficult truth to accept, and even harder to live out. We want to believe that love can climb over any mountain, cross any raging river, rescue from the deepest cavern. It cannot. It does not have that kind of power. Love has the power to persuade, illuminate, and signal, not the power to choose, enlighten, and save. Love is a lighthouse, shining a light to ships buffeted by waves on the stormy sea, warning them of danger, and inviting them home through a safer route. Love is not a rescue boat entering into the waters to save the ship. We want it to be. We would risk it all, we would be that brave and resolute in the storm, but it rarely works that way. The endangered ship can always just sail away, imperiling us in the process. Once we realize, accept, and adapt to our inability to save another soul, to rescue them from themselves, we can embrace our role as a lighthouse: ever vigilant, ever shining, ever ready to welcome them home. Immovable in love, but knowing our role.

Spiritually, Jack also teaches us about the dangers of premature judgment of souls, including our own. Jack feels outside of the reality of grace, feels as though he personifies predestination to darkness, but that reflects his emotional state more than his spiritual state. Often, in daily encounters, he exhibits grace: playing catch with Ames's boy, talking with Lila, helping his father, loving Della. Jack's brooding does not advance his or our knowledge of his spiritual destiny, and his misdeeds do not exhaust his spiritual identity. As readers of the Gilead saga, we have no need to assess the eternal fate of Jack. It is not up to us. There is so much we do not know about how his story might end. Perhaps he finds his way back to his family. Perhaps he has a spiritual awakening, in answer to legions of prayers and years of tears. Perhaps he returns to Gilead with his family and lives a happy life, enjoying Sunday dinners with Lila and her boy and Glory.

Once we realize we need not and cannot judge another soul, we are free to direct our spiritual gaze inward. Judging others easily obscures our own deficiencies as we turn our exacting gaze outward. When we fixate on the real or perceived blemishes of others, we lose the ability to see our own faults clearly. Put simply, judging is spiritual evasion and deflection couched in sanctimony. If we stay busy polishing our own grimy souls we will have work enough for a lifetime. Moreover, once we resign from our self-appointed role of spiritual judge and jury and executioner, we are free to love and enjoy others. We can appreciate their attributes and capacities. We can see their beauty. Glory and Della see the beauty in Jack because their love casts aside judgment. Ames begins to see Jack's beauty when he spiritually pivots from spiritual gatekeeper to spiritual godfather. Jack fails to see the beauty in himself because of his unrelenting self-condemnation.

Lila and *Jack* peer into the background of two beloved characters in the Gilead novels, foregrounding their stories and consciousnesses. Lila's traumas and Jack's troubles engender questions and problems common to the spiritual life. Souls have their own stories and battles that inflect their behavior, sometimes in ways that are spiritually maladaptive. Their dysfunctions do not negate their inherent beauty or dignity, although they can impede their flourishing. Traumatized souls need gentleness, time, and attention. Troubled souls need affirmation, acceptance, and solace. Interaction with these souls, as friends, lovers, or mentors, requires caution and wisdom. Souls embattled by trauma and trouble often fight against those they love because they resist their own happiness. But if we love them deeply and carefully, perhaps they will ultimately receive the grace we all need, the grace they often deny themselves.

Conclusion

As we move through time, we slowly come to terms with our solitude, with the collections of thoughts, experiences, and aspirations that constitute the soul. A surplus always remains just beyond our grasp, an inaccessible mystery. We inhabit our solitudes continually, but we also reach out for companionship. Sometimes the connections are slight and passing, just an episode in the story of our soul. Sometimes, however, they are transformational, reshaping the way we see the world and live in it. Soul companions help us feel at home in the world. Doll, we saw, forms Lila's consciousness, as does Ames, albeit differently. Della forever inhabits Jack's heart, and vice versa. We can have one soul companion or many. They can change over time. What remains constant is this truth: souls inhabit and interpret their solitudes through companionship with other souls, who delicately blow the flame of their soul to life without extinguishing it. Who, I wonder, does that for you?

From these four novels, *Gilead*, *Home*, *Lila*, and *Jack*, we have gleaned many spiritual insights. Unsurprisingly, given the novels' interconnection, many of them intersect. All four novels illustrate the beauty of souls despite their brokenness. They all probe into the nature of suffering.

They all celebrate love in the context of loss and crisis. They all navigate the complex dynamics of solitude and companionship. Other characters, however, deserve further exploration: Ames's grandfather, Teddy, Della, Doll, and many others embed rich spiritual ideas that we could unearth and place alongside our findings. Other concepts from the novels also merit further explication: prayer, preaching, theology, ethics, and so on. The spiritual fecundity of Robinson's novels will ensure further studies of their implications and applications. In these three chapters, I have focused on how they illustrate the beauty of souls and the richness and complexity of the spiritual life.

Notes

1 Marilynne Robinson, *Jack* (New York: Farrar, Straus & Giroux, 2020).

2 "*Lila* turns away from the father–son dynamics of *Gilead* and *Home* to illuminate a minor character through a subjective, inward-looking backstory. . . . *Lila* brings her into center focus, charging her character with complexity and intrigue." Engebretson, *Understanding Marilynne Robinson*, 78.

3 Robinson, *Gilead*, 30, 136–37.

4 "As I have said, I think she experienced a good deal of sorrow in those years. I have never asked, but one thing I have learned in my life is what settled, habitual sadness looks like, and when I saw her I thought, Where have you come from, my dear child?" Robinson, *Gilead*, 136–37. "I ain't what you seem to think I am. I done some things in my life. Like I told you." Marilynne Robinson, *Lila* (New York: Farrar, Straus & Giroux, 2014), 26.

5 Robinson, *Lila*, 7.

6 Robinson, *Lila*, 11.

7 The nature of existence, especially its sharp edges, preoccupies Lila: "That was existence, and why didn't it roar and wrench itself apart

like the storm it must be, if so much of existence is all that bitterness and fear." Robinson, *Lila*, 112. It is never very far from her mind: "Once, when they were out walking, he asked her what was on her mind, because she had been so quiet, and she said, 'Nothing, really. Existence,' which made him laugh with surprise and then apologize for laughing." Robinson, *Lila*, 113.

8 Robinson, *Lila*, 239, 241.

9 Robinson, *Lila*, 23–26.

10 "'You're my wife,' he said. 'I want to take care of you, even if that means someday seeing you to a train." Robinson, *Lila*, 25.

11 "But she would not know how to explain, and if she told him how strange and alone she felt, and wanted to feel, he would wonder why she stayed with him at all." Robinson, *Lila*, 23.

12 Robinson, *Lila*, 92.

13 Robinson, *Gilead*, 149.

14 Tanner, *The Elusive Everyday in the Fiction of Marilynne Robinson*, 129–31.

15 See his tender response to her sharing she worked in a "whorehouse": "She stepped away from him, and he gathered her back and pressed her head against his shoulder. . . . He stroked her hair, and her cheek." Robinson, *Lila*, 89–90.

16 Robinson, *Lila*, 58.

17 Robinson, *Lila*, 253.

18 Robinson, *Lila*, 257.

19 Robinson, *Lila*, 255.

20 For an analysis of the theological dimensions of Lila's question, see Mark S. M. Scott, "Wrestling with Existence: Pondering Suffering and Grace in *Lila*," *Toronto Journal of Theology* 33, no. 2 (2017): 207–17.

21 Robinson, *Lila*, 29.

22 Robinson, *Lila*, 29.

23 Robinson, *Lila*, 59.

24 Robinson, *Lila*, 129.

25 Robinson, *Lila*, 129.

26 Robinson, *Lila*, 87.

27 Robinson, *Lila*, 10.

28 Robinson, *Lila*, 126. Similarly, Jack reflects on his name: "And Jack, which was a name he had for his soul, would even then be falling through uncanny voids and starry abysses toward perdition."

Robinson, *Jack*, 144. But Jack refers to himself and is referred to by many other names: Johnny, Mr. Boughton, J. A. Boughton, Slick, That White Man, the Prince of Darkness, professor, etc. The fluidity of names and their contextual signification runs throughout the Gilead universe.

29 Robinson, *Lila*, 190.

30 Robinson, *Lila*, 182–83.

31 Robinson, *Lila*, 4, 12.

32 Robinson, *Lila*, 70.

33 Robinson, *Lila*, 173–74.

34 Robinson, *Lila*, 241.

35 Robinson, *Lila*, 260; cf. 254.

36 For instance, Jack's "framed photograph of a river" becomes a soul relic simply because Jack liked it, inexplicably. Robinson, *Home*, 285, 322. Once Glory gives it to his son Robert, it becomes a family heirloom. Jack's other soul relic is the small Bible given to him by his father, significantly, by the river. Robinson, *Jack*, 155; cf. Robinson, *Home*, 286. Clearly rivers hold symbolic (perhaps spiritual?) import for Jack. That Bible becomes a thread that tethers him to home, and grace.

37 Robinson, *Lila*, 97.

38 Robinson, *Lila*, 28.

39 Robinson, *Lila*, 258; cf. 110.

40 Robinson, *Lila*, 18.

41 Robinson, *Lila*, 34.

42 Robinson, *Lila*, 56; cf. 81, 253.

43 Robinson, *Lila*, 255.

44 Robinson, *Lila*, 256–57.

45 Robinson, *Gilead*, 50.

46 Robinson, *Lila*, 76–77.

47 Robinson, *Lila*, 255.

48 Robinson, *Lila*, 261.

49 Robinson, *Gilead*, 86–87, 120–23, 125, 141, 160, 164, 173, 188, 211.

50 "Jack Boughton has a wife and a child." Robinson, *Gilead*, 217. Eventually, after a long interior road, he sees his beauty: "On the other hand, he is a man about whom you may never hear one good word, and I just don't know another way to let you see the beauty there is in him." Robinson, *Gilead*, 232.

51 For example, she intervenes when her father ineptly and hurtfully confronts Jack with the death of his young child: "'No. This is terrible. I won't let this happen.' . . . 'That wasn't Jack's fault,' Glory said, 'You know it wasn't.' . . . 'Jack is here now. His life has been hard. It's been sad. And he's home now. He's come home.'" Robinson, *Home*, 295.

52 "Then don't tell me the truth. You've worried us almost to death. You've scared us almost to death. But this [leaving as their father nears death] really is your masterpiece." Robinson, *Home*, 303; cf. *Gilead*, 240.

53 Tanner succinctly captures Jack's complexity: "In *Jack*, her newest novel, she reveals that the black sheep character of the Boughton family, whose troubled past includes theft, imprisonment, alcoholism, and the abandonment of his infant child, is both an avid reader of poetry and a poet." Tanner, *The Elusive Everyday in the Fiction of Marilynne Robinson*, 149.

54 Robinson, *Jack*, 5.

55 Robinson, *Jack*, 9.

56 Robinson, *Jack*, 11, 40, 48, 62, 66, 91, 237, 251. "Constructing himself as the literary or biblical anti-hero, Jack turns himself into the villain of his own tale; no less than seven times in the novel, Jack figures himself as 'The Prince of Darkness' destined to leave a path of destruction in his wake." Tanner, *The Elusive Everyday in the Fiction of Marilynne Robinson*, 153.

57 Jack's retreat into interiority functions simultaneously as reality denialism and reality shaping: "Jack lives largely in his imagination. . . . Throughout *Jack*, Jack's failed attempts to locate himself in the ordinary world are equaled only by his frustrated desire to unrealize his uncomfortable being." Tanner, *The Elusive Everyday in the Fiction of Marilynne Robinson*, 149, 151.

58 Robinson, *Jack*, 37, 39.

59 Robinson, *Jack*, 61.

60 "But I'm basically harmless." Robinson, *Jack*, 70; cf. 119, 153, 207–8, 217.

61 Robinson, *Jack*, 111–16, 188–89.

62 Robinson, *Jack*, 9–79, 184.

63 Robinson, *Jack*, 208.

64 Robinson, *Jack*, 209. Della admires Jack's spiritual authenticity: "I think most people feel a difference between their real lives and the

lives they have in the world. But they ignore their souls, or hide them, so they can keep things together, keep an ordinary life together. You don't do that. In your own way, you're kind of—pure." Robinson, *Jack*, 73. Later, Jack says of Della: "She has a high opinion of my soul." Robinson, *Jack*, 229.

65 Robinson, *Jack*, 94.

66 Robinson, *Jack*, 309.

67 Robinson, *Jack*, 107.

68 Robinson, *Jack*, 125.

69 Robinson, *Jack*, 237.

70 Robinson, *Jack*, 150.

71 Robinson, *Jack*, 185.

72 Robinson, *Jack*, 175.

73 Robinson, *Jack*, 267. "But, what the hell, anyways, he went to Della and put his arms around her . . . he held Della, and he kissed her lips. And she kissed his lips. It was entirely mutual, perfectly simultaneous, he was sure of it. There was no one to blame." Robinson, *Jack*, 178.

74 "And then they embraced, and what an embrace it was, as if they two had survived flood and fire, as if they had solved loneliness. Such an embrace." Robinson, *Jack*, 268.

75 Robinson, *Jack*, 202.

76 Robinson, *Jack*, 155–62, 181.

77 Robinson, *Jack*, 166.

78 Robinson, *Jack*, 166; cf. *Home*, 296.

79 Robinson, *Jack*, 166; cf. *Gilead*, 93, 102.

80 Robinson, *Jack*, 167. On the complexity of the categories of faith and doubt in the Gilead universe, see Mark S. M. Scott, "Faith and Doubt in Gilead: Beyond Spiritual Dichotomies," *Christianity & Literature* 70, no. 2 (2021): 142–52.

81 Robinson, *Jack*, 43; cf. *Home*, 277.

Conclusion

> I swear to you there are divine things
> more beautiful than words can tell.
>
> —Walt Whitman, "Song of the Open Road"

I have identified the beauty of souls as the unifying, organizing, and defining concept of Robinson's writing, both fiction and nonfiction. Robinson vigorously defends the beauty of souls against contemporary reductionistic paradigms in her nonfiction, while depicting the beauty of souls in her fiction. They are twin aspects of her rehabilitative attempt to recapture the brilliance of humanity in an age of simplistic "scientific" storylines and leveling "philosophical" ontologies. We are so much more than any mundane theory of the human person. We are capable of so much more than today's narrow anthropologies allow. Like a rancher who cruelly confines a stallion to its stall, keeping it from roaming free, pseudo-scientists want to pen in the soul, to deny it or artificially define its parameters. Robinson wants to unbridle the human soul, to let it run free in wide-open fields, to let it discover new ranges and exhibit its hidden power and beauty.

The beauty of souls, then, is the hermeneutical lens through which I have read her diverse body of work. As a literary lens, the beauty of souls provides an intelligible guide to her writings, where she "sings" of the beauty of life and the majesty of souls in different registers. As a spiritual lens, the beauty of souls invites readers to discover and rediscover themselves as souls and the world around them as beautiful. Its spiritual fecundity lies precisely in its ability to awaken, enliven, and activate souls. Its generative impact will be as diverse as the souls that encounter her fictional worlds and perceive their hidden magic. Robinson's writings make room for a plurality of perspectives and multitude of meanings, so I would expect other readers to glean other, sometimes contrary, spiritual insights from her works. I have not attempted the definitive spiritual guide to her work, but rather have offered a way into her writings that might be theoretically and spiritually productive.

The unwavering focus on beauty, however, does not obscure the brokenness of the world. Her nonfiction does not shy away from the challenges facing humanity, including political polarization, social injustice, and environmental disaster. Likewise, her fiction faces the real harm done by its characters. Helen's suicide leaves her daughters in a precarious situation. Jack's abandonment of his first child contributed to her early death. Robinson's characters inhabit worlds rife with violence, injustice, and exploitation. To affirm the beauty of souls downplays neither the world's capacity for harm, nor its darkness. The world still awaits redemption in her fiction and nonfiction, but she sounds hopeful notes that souls can recover their beauty and work toward a more beautiful world. In theological terms, fallen souls, though marred, still bear the image of God, still have the capacity to shine forth God's love. Even ruined castles retain their splendor.

When we meet a fellow soul, we encounter a miracle, the culmination and collision of cosmic and terrestrial forces. God spoke and the cosmos unfurled in ways we cannot grasp: light out of darkness, order out of chaos, abundance out of emptiness. Life appears within this fragile incubation, a pocket of life amid an inhospitable immensity: "Say that we are a puff of warm breath in a very cold universe."[1] Life begins, mistakes and promises are made, societies form, and souls navigate the ebbs and flow of existence. We will never know the chance meetings, hard decisions, unforeseen circumstances, and unheralded lives that eventuated in the person before us. They are a miracle, a mystery, a whisper from the past, an ambassador of lost generations. In them live the forgotten hopes and dreams of their unknown ancestors, and through them countless new generations of souls will spiral out like Abraham's stars.[2] It is staggering to capture a glimpse of a soul.

But the majesty, magnitude, and miracle of their very existence quickly fades from our consciousness in the flow of life. Souls do pedestrian things: sleep, wash, eat, work, and play. And they do not always actualize their lofty spiritual potential: they lie, cheat, exploit, and fail. We lose sight of the miracle of souls in the mundane, fallen world. Robinson, in her fiction and nonfiction, calls attention to what we so easily forget. As we slowly internalize the beauty of her characters, we undergo a subtle spiritual transformation. We see with more clarity and vibrancy the beauty of the natural world, the beauty of relationships, and even the beauty hidden in brokenness. Robinson spiritually sensitizes us to the beauty within us and the beauty around us. She encourages us to embrace ourselves and others as beautiful souls. She elicits from the soul its own song, with its complex interplay of joy and sorrow, and invites us to sing it. Too often we stay silent for fear of singing out of tune.

Robinson stirs the soul. She does not, however, create her own spirituality. She is not a founder of a school of spirituality. There is no "Robinsonian spirituality" that delineates spiritual disciplines for an intentional community. Rather, she softens the soil of the soul, quietly plants seeds, and lets the flowers bloom. Her fiction prepares for the spiritual life—*praeparatio spiritualitas*—it does not promote a particular version of it. Her subjective spiritual sensibilities, influenced by American transcendentalism, preclude a community rule: each soul must find its own way home in the end. And yet, despite her individual orientation, she affirms the vital importance of community in her novels and in her essays. Communities must mobilize not for the sake of the community but for the sake of the souls they serve. Moreover, her spiritual instincts and sensibilities can serve spiritual communities seeking to deepen their spiritual life.

In summary, Robinson's writings spiritually awaken, activate, and sensitize her readers, at least those interested in the life of the soul. Souls matter because they are the deep, mysterious essence of the self: the dynamic synthesis of our thoughts, experiences, hopes, dreams, abilities, and aspirations, as well as the culmination of the cosmic and personal forces that are inscribed into their very fabric. Robinson's writings invite us to acknowledge the soul—ours and others—and to value it. They recommend a spirit of openness to others where we respect their otherness and the mystery of their existence. Her novels teach us to slow down and attend to the surprising ways beauty breaks into everyday life. Beauty abounds all around us: in nature, in relationships, in art, in thought, in the daily rhythms of life. We have only to train our spiritual eyes to see the abundance of beauty awaiting our notice. Her writings help us to do that. Deep calls to deep.

Notes

1 Robinson, *When I Was a Child I Read Books*, 36.

2 "God sees, through Abram's eyes, beauty that might seem an arbitrary display of divine power if it were only a throng of stars." Robinson, *Reading Genesis*, 98; cf. 220.

Bibliography

Augustine. *The Confessions*. 2nd ed. Translated by Maria Boulding. Edited by John E. Rotelle. New York: New City Press, 2012.

Ávila, Teresa. *Interior Castle*. Edited and translated by E. Allison Peers. New York: Dover Publications, 2007.

Barton, Emily. "Slowly but Surely." *Los Angeles Times*, September 7, 2008. https://www.latimes.com/archives/la-xpm-2008-sep-07-ca-marilynne-robinson7-story.html.

Coogan, Michael D., ed. *The New Oxford Annotated Bible: New Revised Standard Version with the Apocrypha*. 5th ed. Oxford: Oxford University Press, 2018.

Crisu, Corina. "At Home with Transience: Reconfiguring Female Characters of the American West in Marilynne Robinson's *Housekeeping*." In *This Life, This World: New Essays on Marilynne Robinson's "Housekeeping," "Gilead," and "Home,"* edited by Jason W. Stevens, 38–58. Leiden: Brill, 2015.

Cunning, Andrew. *Marilynne Robinson, Theologian of the Ordinary*. New York: Bloomsbury Academic, 2021.

Engebretson, Alex. *Understanding Marilynne Robinson*. Columbia: The University of South Carolina Press, 2017.

Fay, Sarah, "Marilynne Robinson: The Art of Fiction no. 198." *Paris Review* 186 (2008). https://www.theparisreview.org/interviews/5863/the-art-of-fiction-no-198-marilynne-robinson.

Hoezee, Scott. "A World of Beautiful Souls: An Interview with Marilynne Robinson." *The Reformed Journal*, May 16, 2005. https://reformedjournal.com/a-world-of-beautiful-souls-an-interview-with-marilynne-robinson/.

Larsen, Timothy, and Keith L. Johnson, eds. *Balm in Gilead: A Theological Dialogue*. Downers Grove, IL: InterVarsity Press, 2019.

Mariotti, Shannon L., and Joseph H. Lane Jr. "Introduction: The Mystery of Experience: Marilynne Robinson's Political Theory." In *A Political Companion to Marilynne Robinson*, edited by Shannon L. Mariotti and Joseph H. Lane Jr., 1–17. Lexington: The University Press of Kentucky, 2016.

Mason, Wyatt Mason. "The Revelations of Marilynne Robinson." *The New York Times Magazine*, October 1, 2014. https://www.nytimes.com/2014/10/05/magazine/the-revelations-of-marilynne-robinson.html.

Merton, Thomas. *Conjectures of a Guilty Bystander*. New York: Image Books, 2009. First published 1966.

Pym, John. "Production Report." Insert in *Housekeeping*. Directed by Bill Forsyth. Culver City, CA: Columbia Pictures, 1987. Blu-ray DVD.

Robinson, Marilynne. *Absence of Mind: The Dispelling of Inwardness from the Modern Myth of the Self.* New Haven, CT: Yale University Press, 2010.

Robinson, Marilynne. *The Death of Adam: Essays on Modern Thought*. New York: Picador, 1998.

Robinson, Marilynne. *Gilead*. New York: Farrar, Straus & Giroux, 2004.

Robinson, Marilynne. *The Givenness of Things*. New York: Farrar, Straus & Giroux, 2015.

Robinson, Marilynne. *Home*. New York: Farrar, Straus & Giroux, 2008.

Robinson, Marilynne. *Housekeeping*. New York: Farrar, Straus & Giroux, 1980.

Robinson, Marilynne. *Jack*. New York: Farrar, Straus & Giroux, 2020.
Robinson, Marilynne. *Lila*. New York: Farrar, Straus & Giroux, 2014.
Robinson, Marilynne. *Mother Country: Britain, the Welfare State and Nuclear Pollution*. New York: Farrar, Straus & Giroux, 1989.
Robinson, Marilynne. *Reading Genesis*. New York: Farrar, Straus & Giroux, 2024.
Robinson, Marilynne. *What Are We Doing Here?* New York: Farrar, Straus & Giroux, 2018.
Robinson, Marilynne. *When I Was a Child I Read Books*. New York: Farrar, Straus & Giroux, 2012.
Ruse, Michael. *Atheism: What Everyone Needs to Know*. Oxford: Oxford University Press, 2015.
Schaub, Thomas. "An Interview with Marilynne Robinson." *Contemporary Literature* 35 (1994): 231–51.
Scott, A. O. "Return of the Prodigal Son." *New York Times*, September 21, 2008. https://www.nytimes.com/2008/09/21/books/review/Scott-t.html.
Scott, Mark S. M. "Beauty from Ashes: Aesthetic Transformations of Suffering in *Gilead*." *CRUX* 52, no. 3/4 (2016): 11–18.
Scott, Mark S. M. "In the Face of Mystery: Soteriological Symbolism in *Gilead* and *Home*." In *This Life, This World: New Essays on Marilynne Robinson's "Housekeeping," "Gilead," and "Home,"* edited by Jason W. Stevens, 148–70. Leiden: Brill, 2015.
Scott, Mark S. M. "Faith and Doubt in Gilead: Beyond Spiritual Dichotomies." *Christianity & Literature* 70, no. 2 (2021): 142–52.
Scott, Mark S. M. "Souls in the Dark: Theodicy and Domesticity in *Home*." *Religions* 8, no. 273 (2017): 1–6.
Scott, Mark S. M. "Wrestling with Existence: Pondering Suffering and Grace in *Lila*." *Toronto Journal of Theology* 33, no. 2 (2017): 207–17.
Shakespeare, William. *Hamlet*. Edited by G. R. Hibbard. Oxford World's Classics. Oxford: Oxford University Press, 2008.
Tanner, Laura E. *The Elusive Everyday in the Fiction of Marilynne Robinson*. New York: Oxford University Press, 2021.
Whitman, Walt. "Song of the Open Road." In *Leaves of Grass*, 222. Cleveland: Duke Classics, 2012.

Index